Praise for Femme Led

Femme Led: Hard-Learned Lessons from Women in Leadership is a powerful anthology that redefines leadership through the lived experiences of women, showcasing their resilience, authenticity, and transformative journeys. Through personal stories, the book challenges traditional leadership norms and inspires readers to embrace their unique strengths and lead with integrity, vulnerability, and courage.

I see a lot of similarities with many of the stories that parallel my journey.

— **Dawn Tiura**, President and CEO of SIG.org, SIG University and the Future of Sourcing

Femme Led is not a manual on leadership; it is a mirror. Through lived truth and courageous honesty, these women illuminate a path where care and ferocity, intuition and strategy, can coexist and where leading as women becomes our greatest strength.

— **Heidi Richards Mooney**, Author, Speaker & Leadership Advocate & Publisher, *Women of Wisdom Magazine*

Raw, honest and authentic in the best possible way. Reading this book feels like being invited inside someone's mind. As the stories unfold, you recognize pieces of your own journey and feel seen and deeply understood. The wisdom shared throughout is powerful and incredibly inspiring, leaving you reflecting on what might be possible for your own leadership path.

— **Joanna Kaniewska**, PhD, Founder T-Shaped

Femme Led is a rare kind of leadership book—one that replaces formulas with lived truth. Through deeply personal stories of risk, reinvention, and integrity, these women show that real leadership begins the moment you stop contorting to fit and start honoring what you know to be true.

— **Naeem Zafar,** Professor, Author and Tech Entrepreneur, CEO coach and Advisor

Femme Led captures a truth about leadership that many books miss: it is a messy, courageous path of learning, adapting, and trusting your voice to emerge over time. The women in these pages share their journeys with a level of vulnerability and hindsight that becomes a gift to any woman who wonders when she will finally arrive. At times, they challenge us to dare to differ, and to embrace who we are meant to become. I found these stories both grounding and inspiring and would recommend this book to any woman asking herself what leadership might look like on her own terms.

— **Barbara Koenig**, CEO Impact3Leadership

Femme Led

Hard-Learned Lessons from Women in Leadership

Sierra Melcher   Carol Britton

Janice Marquardt   Donna Marie Marino

Tracy Macdonald   Anna Dravland

Tiffany Harris   Jean Smarto   Diana Frank

Catalina Escobar Bravo   Asya Dimitrova

Michelle McCartney   Stephanie Mikulasek

Ann McCreath   Alexandra Yung

Dr. Katherine Humphreys

RED THREAD BOOKS

In memory of Carolina Gaviria;
A young leader, guardian of the jaguar, keeper of a Colombia worth
protecting. You are gone too soon, but your work moves through the
forests, and your message lives on in every life you touched.
www.expedicionjaguar.com/english

Contents

Foreword — xi
—Sierra Melcher

Introduction — xv
—Stephanie Mikulasek

1. THE LEADERSHIP LEAP — 1
—Sierra Melcher & Stephanie Mikulasek

2. HOW RESILIENCY DRIVES PURPOSE — 19
—Catalina Escobar Bravo

3. DESPITE THE FEAR — 29
—Carol Britton

4. A SPIDER WEB IN A STORM — 39
—Anna Dravland

5. BECOMING BRAVE — 45
—Tracy Macdonald

6. CORPORATE ENTREPRENEUR — 59
—Janice Marquardt

7. I BEG YOU TO DIFFER — 71
—Diana Frank

8. GRIT-TO-GRACE — 85
—Dr. Katherine Humphreys

9. THE EPIDURAL BLINDED ME — 97
—Donna Marie Marino

10. FIRE THAT BITCH — 107
—Jean Smarto

11. ABANDONING THE SCRIPT — 117
—Michelle McCartney

12. THE UN-ABANDONABLE MISSION — 127
—Asya Dimitrova

13. THE POWER OF SAYING YES — 137
—Tiffany Harris

14. INVESTING IN ART 147
—Ann McCreath

15. BEYOND TRANSACTIONS 157
—Alexandra Yung

Thank You 167
Acknowledgments 169
Red Thread Books 171
Other Books 173

Publisher's Note

Femme Led brings together authors from around the world. To honor each contributor's voice and regional identity, we have preserved original spellings rather than standardizing to British or American English.

We have also maintained each author's chosen language and tone. As such, readers may encounter occasional strong language, reflective of authentic lived experience.

This anthology represents a collection of individual perspectives. Each author is solely responsible for the views expressed in her chapter; those views do not necessarily reflect those of the publisher.

Foreword
At the Threshold
—Sierra Melcher

We didn't sit down to define leadership. We sat down to talk. Not as experts delivering answers, not as women who had it all figured out, but as two people (Stephanie & Sierra) thinking out loud together, listening for what was true beneath the roles, the resumés, or the titles. Again and again, the same tension surfaced. Leadership, as we had been taught, was about control.

About mitigating risk.

About managing outcomes.

About staying in the head, overriding what the body already knew.

That model worked, until it didn't.

At some point, each of us reached a moment where the old structure stopped holding. The plan imploded. The strategy stopped working. There was no panic, just a quiet clarity: *we couldn't keep doing it this way.* What emerged instead was something harder to name and easier to feel. Leadership, we realized, is not about controlling the outcome.

It's about being a vehicle, letting the energy flow through.

It's about holding the container, not forcing the result.

It's about trust.

It's about allowing emergence.

It's about letting people be themselves.

So much of what actually makes leadership work has been dismissed as "intangible." And yet, many of us learned to override our instincts, our gut feelings, our sense of what was needed.

We learned to contort ourselves to fit structures that were never designed with our full humanity in mind. We learned to separate being a woman from being a leader, as if those were incompatible identities. We learned to shrink, smooth, soften, or harden, as required, to survive. This book exists because something in us refused that split.

- What if leadership didn't require us to erase ourselves?
- What if leadership could include care and ferocity, rest and rigor, intuition and strategy?
- What if leadership wasn't a performance, but a practice of integrity?

The women in these pages are not offering theories. They are offering lived truths. Each chapter is like a keynote delivered from experience: hard-earned, embodied, and honest. Together, they expand the definition of leadership beyond titles and ladders, into the places where real decisions are made: homes, bodies, businesses, communities, and moments of profound change. This anthology is not here to tell you how to lead.

It is here to help you recognize yourself.

You will see your questions reflected here.

You will feel your edge named.

You may even recognize the quiet knowing that has been trying to get your attention.

If you are standing at a threshold, if something old no longer fits and something new has not yet fully formed, know this:

You are not behind.
You are not broken.
You are not alone.

Leadership, as these women show us, begins not with certainty, but with truth. And telling the truth, together, is where the leap begins.

Introduction
—Stephanie Mikulasek

THE LANDSCAPE WOMEN NAVIGATE

There is a moment that doesn't look dramatic from the outside. Nothing is on fire. Nothing has fallen apart in a way that requires an emergency response. On paper, things look fine. But inside, something has shifted.

It's quiet. Subtle. Persistent.

Your body knows before your mind catches up. You feel it in the exhaustion that rest doesn't fix. In the sense that the role you're playing no longer fits the person you've become. In the way success starts to feel strangely hollow, not because you failed, but because you outgrew it. This moment is happening to women everywhere. Quietly. Persistently. And it's asking something of us.

WHAT'S DIFFERENT ABOUT WOMEN'S LEADERSHIP

For generations, women have been taught to lead *despite* being women, not *as* women. The inherited model of leadership, the one most of us absorbed through observation, education, and organizational culture, was built on control. Control of outcomes. Control of risk.

Control of perception. It privileges logic over intuition, certainty over curiosity, performance over truth. It asks us to stay in our heads, to manage and mitigate, to override what our bodies already know. This model works until it doesn't.

What gets dismissed in this framework are the very things that make leadership sustainable and human: intuition, somatic knowing, care, timing, and the capacity to hold space for emergence. These qualities don't spreadsheet well. They can't be measured in quarterly reports. They resist reduction to metrics. So we learned to treat them as optional. Indulgent, even.

But anyone who has actually led through uncertainty knows the opposite is true. The intangible is not soft. It is foundational. It is where truth lives. The cost of ignoring this has been steep.

Women perform competence while disconnecting from wholeness. We succeed by fragmenting ourselves: the professional mask here, the intuitive knower tucked away there, the caregiver apologizing for needing her own space, the strategist pretending the body's signals don't matter.

We achieve, and we burn out.

We advance, and we lose ourselves.

We lead, but at the expense of our humanity.

What we are reclaiming now, what the women in this book are modeling, is leadership that doesn't require self-erasure.

Leadership as a container, not control.

Leadership as integrity, not performance.

Leadership that trusts emergence instead of demanding certainty.

Leadership that includes the fullness of who we are: the care and the ferocity, the rest and the rigor, the intuition and the strategy.

THE PATTERN WE KEEP SEEING: THE LEADERSHIP LEAP

As we spoke with the women whose voices fill these pages, a pattern emerged. Again and again, we heard about a moment, a rupture, not a plan, when the old system stopped working.

The strategy failed.

The structure collapsed.

The model that had carried them this far suddenly couldn't hold the person they were becoming. And instead of panic, there was clarity. A quiet, undeniable knowing: *I can't keep doing it this way.*

This is what we've come to call a leadership leap. Not a promotion. Not a carefully plotted career move. Not a five-year plan executed flawlessly. A leap is what happens when the misalignment between how you've been leading and what is actually true becomes unbearable.

It doesn't look dramatic. It looks honest. It's the executive who walks away from the corner office because something inside her finally said *enough*. It's the entrepreneur who burns down her entire business model because she refuses to keep performing a version of success that requires hiding. It's the mother who stops apologizing for needing rest and starts building her life around what's actually sustainable. It's the writer who finally publishes the truth she's been carrying for years, even though it terrifies her.

Leaps happen when we stop overriding ourselves. When we stop contorting to fit. When we let the body's knowing become louder than the inherited script.

You'll see this pattern woven through many chapters of this book, in different forms, across industries and life stages. Some women will name it explicitly. Others will embody it without using the language. But the thread is there: a refusal to keep leading in ways that fragment, diminish, or erase.

WHY CONFIDENCE COMES AFTER, NOT BEFORE

One of the most persistent myths about leadership is that it requires confidence. That you act from a place of knowing. That certainty precedes the decision.

But women who have taken leadership leaps will tell you

something different. Confidence comes *after* the leap, not before it. There is no perfect moment. No clean plan. No guarantee that you'll land safely.

Most meaningful leaps happen without metrics, without external validation, without the comfort of certainty. They happen because staying where you are, continuing to override your truth, continuing to fragment yourself, continuing to perform leadership at the expense of your humanity, hurts more than the unknown ahead.

This is where the model we were taught breaks down entirely. We've been conditioned to wait. To gather more credentials. To prove ourselves ready. To mitigate every possible risk before we move. But readiness is a myth designed to keep us waiting.

The leap requires something else entirely: trust in emergence. Trust that the path will reveal itself as you walk it. Trust that you don't need to know the outcome before you begin. This is where the intangible becomes non-negotiable.

You can't control your way into a leap. You can't logic your way through it. You have to feel your way forward, listening to what your body knows, trusting what your intuition whispers, holding space for what wants to emerge.

This is not reckless. This is honest. And honesty, it turns out, is the most radical form of leadership available to us.

WHAT YOU'LL FIND IN THESE PAGES

Each woman in this book has stood at an edge. Some have leaped. Some are standing at the threshold right now, feeling the pull and the fear in equal measure. Some have leaped multiple times, knowing that the leap is not a destination but a way of being. Their industries are different. Their paths are different. The specific edges they face are different. But the refusal is the same.

The refusal to erase themselves.

The refusal to perform leadership at the expense of their humanity.

The refusal to keep quiet about what they know.

You will find chapters that name your exact question—the one you've been carrying quietly, wondering if anyone else feels this way. You will find chapters that show you edges you haven't reached yet, giving you language for something you've sensed but couldn't articulate. You will find chapters that challenge you, that make you uncomfortable, that ask you to look at the places where you're still contorting to fit. And through it all, you will find a truth that runs deeper than any single story:

Wholeness is not optional. It's the point. Leadership that requires you to fragment, diminish, or hide is not leadership. It's survival. And survival is not the same as thriving.

The women in these pages are thriving, not in spite of being women, but *as* women. Not by overriding their humanity, but by leading from it.

Chapter 1
The Leadership Leap
A Dialogue
—Sierra Melcher & Stephanie Mikulasek

SIERRA: Hi.

> STEPHANIE: So, hi. How are you?

SIERRA: I am pretty exuberant, actually.

> STEPHANIE: I love exuberant.

This is how the conversation began: two women in different time zones, life happening all around them, settling in to explore a question that has haunted and called to us both: What does it mean to be a leader and to be a woman, not separately, but simultaneously?

Not a "female leader." A leader. Full stop. And someone who happens to have lady parts, as well as the heart, mind, and socialization that make us women. Doing both things at the same time.

We chose a dialogue format for this chapter because it felt genuinely feminine, uniquely nonhierarchical. We learn in a dialogue. We trust our instincts and we co-create. Most of the chapters that follow are single-person presentations, in a keynote-style voice, sharing their truths. But we wanted to set a different tone here, to show you what happens when two women come together to think out loud, to hold space for each other, to let the conversation unfold. This was our third call, but it felt like we'd been doing this forever.

THE LEADERSHIP WE WERE TAUGHT

SIERRA: Becoming a leader, I tried on all the "leader things" that didn't fit. I tried all the ways I perceived leaders needed to be, which were much more masculine. However, forcing myself into a shape of leadership that wasn't, that didn't fit, was absolutely the recipe for burnout, disappointment, and inauthenticity.

I grew up watching Working Girl in the '80s. I thought that to be a leader, I needed to be more like a man.

STEPHANIE: Absolutely. Last week in Guatemala, I met this amazing indigenous woman who led us through a Mayan ceremony at a sacred lake. I was going through this experience, my head processing and analyzing, until something in me said stop, just be here. So I let myself be really there, fully present in that space. And after a while, this realization shows up. That, as a leader, thinking the work is to control outcomes and mitigate risk and measure metrics is totally wrong. It was a thought that wasn't cerebral, it was something I felt. It was this sense: Stephanie, just let yourself be the vehicle through which the energy flows. You're not here to control this. You're here to let it flow.

Earlier we were talking about leadership not being about control; it's about being the container. Holding the space and letting the magic happen and unfold. It's about valuing both the metric and the intention, the measurable and the intangible. We've overlooked the intangible for centuries because we can't name it, can't measure it, can't weigh it. Does that mean it's not valuable? We think it's *invaluable*.

This is what we call the "intellectual override." That moment when we notice the instinct, consider it, and then override it. Or worse, when the voice has been silenced for so long that it doesn't even register in the process because it's not logical, not practical, not measurable.

> SIERRA: How many of us have said to ourselves later: "I just knew that wasn't the right call"?

> STEPHANIE: Exactly. And that's where our leadership leaps begin; when we stop trying to fit the model and start trusting what we know and what we sense – our intuition.

WHAT IS A LEADERSHIP LEAP?

> STEPHANIE: A leap moment is when the system, the playbook, you've been operating in, no longer aligns with what's true. It's a rupture. Not a plan. Not a promotion. It's a fundamental misalignment that becomes impossible to ignore.

> SIERRA: It's that moment when staying where you are hurts more than the unknown ahead. And here's what surprised me: there's usually no panic. Just this strange, calm clarity.

> STEPHANIE: Yes. The clarity is what catches people off guard. They expect drama. Fire. Collapse. But it's quieter than that. It's just: "I can't keep doing it this way."

> SIERRA: And it's not a one-time thing. We've both had more than a baker's dozen of these moments.

> STEPHANIE: More than a baker's dozen, absolutely. Because the leap isn't a destination. It's an emergence. A way of being.

SIERRA: There's an anatomy to it, if we're being honest. There's the before: the restlessness, the misalignment, the exhaustion that rest doesn't fix. Then there's the edge: the moment of recognition. Your body knows. It's somatic. You can't think your way out of it.

STEPHANIE: Then the leap itself, letting go. Trusting emergence, the unfolding. Becoming the container instead of trying to control the outcome.

SIERRA: And after, integration. Wholeness. Leadership that doesn't require you to erase yourself.

STEPHANIE: And it's not linear. You don't leap once and you're done. It cycles. Each time you outgrow a container, you'll feel the edge again.

SIERRA: Which is both terrifying and weirdly comforting.

OUR LEAP MOMENTS

SIERRA: My most recent one: I had to completely restructure my team, strip everything back to the beginning. My daughter entered two months of vacation, and I was exhausted and emotionally burnt. So I went into a cave, and I knew that I needed to rest with a vengeance.

I would deprioritize work and watch Netflix all afternoon, listen to an audiobook all the way through, eight hours straight; just done. But there was no panic in it; I didn't know how long it would last, but I knew it would end.

I knew what I needed, and I knew there was something on the other side.

And then the energy had been restored. The
clarity of direction presented itself, and the
people arrived. I wasn't faking anymore. I
was exactly who I was, and it was the game-
changer.

> STEPHANIE: When my job imploded, there
> was no more Agency to work for. All the plans
> were just gone, including retirement. And
> when I dove into launching my company, I
> had no idea where it would go. I just knew
> that I needed to do this. I didn't have a
> proper three- to five-year business plan with
> financial metrics. I just knew I was going to
> start.
>
> I've been amazed at the number of women
> with whom I've shared my vision and offered
> only this: I can't pay you, but come aboard.
> Let's create this.
>
> And they all said yes.
>
> That's the magic of it. When you stop
> performing and start being real, people show
> up and respond.

SIERRA: There's a story at the beginning of
Women Who Run with Wolves about the
bone woman. She wanders the desert
collecting bones. She looks like a crazy
person. But she brings the bones together,
and through some kind of magic, they
eventually come to life and run through the
desert.

That's what it feels like. We're picking up
things that are dead, and we're making
something alive, and it doesn't make sense,
and it's contrary to a lot of the things we
think about the way the world is supposed to
work, but it happens anyway.

> STEPHANIE: Is it any odder than spending sixteen hours a day working behind a computer, ignoring our kids, our health, our well-being, day after day, for what? For the sake of what?

SIERRA: Exactly. We'd much rather, literally, wander the desert.

THE HARDEST PART: IDENTITY SHIFT

SIERRA: Here's the thing nobody talks about: the identity shift required to take a leadership leap is massive. It's not just changing what you do. It's changing who you are. And that feels like putting on a jacket that doesn't quite fit.

> STEPHANIE: You're stepping into something new before you feel ready. Before it feels natural.

SIERRA: I worked with a ghostwriter once who had written multiple international bestsellers. Bestsellers! And she didn't claim that identity. She didn't tell anyone. I asked her, "What does your email signature say?" And she said, "Just my name."

I said, "Update it. Right now. Put 'International Bestselling Author.'"

She did. Within a month, she had three new clients.

> STEPHANIE: Because she finally allowed herself to be what she already was.

SIERRA: Exactly. The identity shift is the leap. Not the accomplishment. The claiming.

STEPHANIE: I had to do this when I shifted from diplomat to entrepreneur. From corporate to creative. Everything I knew about leadership came from hierarchical systems. Titles. Org charts. Clear lines of authority.

And suddenly I'm building something without those structures. Where leadership means holding space rather than dictating outcomes. Where my value isn't tied to a title someone gave me; it's tied to courage, asking for help, and my willingness to show up fully.

That was terrifying.

SIERRA: What did you have to let go of?

STEPHANIE: Certainty. The illusion that if I planned hard enough, I could control the outcome. The belief that my worth was tied to external validation.

And honestly? I had to let go of the version of myself who needed everyone to approve of my decisions. And by the way, my company's name is The ServantEDGE. Part of the meaning of "edge" is that moment of discomfort, when you can no longer go back and unsee what you realize now, and so you take that leap.

SIERRA: That's the hardest one.

STEPHANIE: What about you? What did you have to let go of?

SIERRA: The idea that I had to have it all figured out before I could lead. The belief that leadership meant knowing all the answers. The mask of competence was exhausting me.

I had to let go of the version of myself who thought being vulnerable was weak.

STEPHANIE: And what did you refuse to compromise?

SIERRA: My truth. My voice. The messy, imperfect, dyslexic reality of who I am. I refused to keep pretending I was someone else just to make other people comfortable.

STEPHANIE: That's the shift. You don't become a leader. You allow yourself to be one. You stop performing and start inhabiting.

WRITING AS A LEADERSHIP LEAP

STEPHANIE: For a lot of women, writing is where the leadership leap becomes visible. It's the first public act of claiming authority without permission.

SIERRA: Because writing forces the identity shift. You can't write under a pen name and hide forever. At some point, you have to attach your name to your words. Your ideas. Your truth.

And that can be paralyzing.

STEPHANIE: The professionals I work with, executives, leaders, people with incredible expertise, they all say the same thing: "What if people read this? What if my friends see it? What if my boss thinks I'm..."

SIERRA: Out of line. Overstepping. Too much.

STEPHANIE: Exactly. The fear isn't really about writing. It's about being seen. Fully. Without the professional mask.

SIERRA: Writing is integrity on the page. It's the alignment between what's true internally and what you're willing to make visible externally. What you will fiercely claim by putting it into the world for all to see.

And that requires a leap.

> STEPHANIE: It's not that different from any other leadership leap, actually. You're stepping into a new identity - author, thought leader, public voice - before it feels comfortable. Before you feel ready.

SIERRA: And you're doing it knowing there's no guarantee anyone will care. No guarantee it'll be well-received. No guarantee you won't be criticized or dismissed.

> STEPHANIE: But you do it anyway. Because silence is no longer an option.

SIERRA: That's the leap.

> STEPHANIE: When the cost of not speaking becomes higher than the cost of being seen.

SIERRA: And when you take that leap, when you publish, when you put your name on your ideas, you're not just writing. You're leading. You're saying, "This matters. I matter. And I'm not waiting for permission to say so."

WHO WE ARE

SIERRA: We should probably tell people who we are.

> STEPHANIE: Oh, right. The credentials.

SIERRA: You first.

STEPHANIE: I briefly worked in the Silicon Valley, spent 18 years in the diplomatic corps, including the Department of State and mostly USAID, co-owned a leadership development company, and worked in both nonprofit leadership and academia. I'm a certified Executive Coach, hold a couple of master's degrees, and soon will finish my doctorate - I'm pretty much a lifelong student – while raising two phenomenal daughters, both now in university. After closing my former company, I founded The ServantEDGE based on a mission I wrote in Puebla, Mexico in 2004: build bridges of understanding and compassion while tearing down walls of prejudice and fear.

My greatest fear is that we seem to be pummeling in the other direction.

SIERRA: I run a publishing company helping people, especially women, write and publish impactful nonfiction to change the world. I'm dyslexic. I have a master's degree in education. I'm a single parent raising my daughter alone. I've lived abroad for twenty years.

I do this work because of the integration; the interplay between writing and leadership, the identity transformation that happens when emotional work meets visible accomplishment. Witnessing and supporting women, especially as they step into the fullness of their being, comes from the emotional heavy lifting we do to get to a final draft. We are different at the end than we were when we came to the process. This transformation, this integration, is what I live for.

So underneath it all, we both just give a damn.

STEPHANIE: Exactly right – that's our superpower.

SIERRA: And maybe we suffer from what we call "proximity blindness."

STEPHANIE: Proximity blindness?

SIERRA: We're so close to our own experiences that we can't see them. We assume everyone knows what we know because it's so obvious to us.

Women especially. We downplay everything. The master's degrees, the doctorates, the million certificates and phenomenal knowledge. As soon as we know something, we think everyone knows it. We don't recognize the value of our own understanding.

STEPHANIE: I can't tell you how many times I've talked with other women about this, how much we minimize our expertise. I do this. We let ourselves play small; we implicitly apologize for taking up space.

SIERRA: Which is why the leap matters.

STEPHANIE: Because the leap is the moment we stop minimizing and start claiming.

LOVE LETTERS TO WOMEN AT THE EDGE

STEPHANIE: If you're standing at your edge right now, if you're reading this and feeling that quiet recognition in your chest, I want to say this to you:

All that you need is within yourself.

There is nothing that needs to be fixed within you. Nothing. You are whole and complete in who you are.

I see too many women mired in stress or worry or procrastination or not good enough or all the things, and all that muck sits between here and there - whatever the "there" is for you. The point is not thinking those feelings will go away - the point is to leap over them and do it anyway, because you are completely whole just as you are.

To the dear person reading: Allow yourself to embrace this truth. Get to know the wise woman within you. There is a sisterhood holding a safe space, a container that will nourish you, and be with you. Let the most feminine parts of you show up and be validated and affirmed by yourself first, and then by others.

SIERRA: I'm going to agree and completely contradict you.

STEPHANIE: I love that.

SIERRA: The greatest obstacle to this vision was my old way of operating. Granting myself this gift felt impossible.

So I've hacked it.

I can harness our caregiving, our kindness, our ferocity when I focus on who needs me.

Tell me somebody needs me? Forget all that other stuff. I don't care if it's not possible. I don't care if I can't fly. I'm going to fly to the top of the mountain anyway. Back up 'cause I'm about to go.

STEPHANIE: That's beautiful.

SIERRA: Sometimes that first step to believe in yourself is the hardest thing. So don't start there. Focus on who needs you. Let the motivation and intuition guide you. You'll still get there anyway.

STEPHANIE: Two blessings. Take whichever one you need.

SIERRA: Are you a leader because you started a company, or did you start a company because you're a leader?

STEPHANIE: Does the order matter?

THE INVITATION

STEPHANIE: If you're standing at your edge, know this: the leap doesn't require knowing where you'll land.

SIERRA: It only requires telling the truth, first to yourself.

STEPHANIE: And then, when you're ready, to the world.

SIERRA: The leap is not loud. It's not dramatic. It doesn't announce itself.

STEPHANIE: It's honest.

SIERRA: And it begins the moment you decide to stop pretending you don't feel the edge.

STEPHANIE: Whether you find your way by recognizing you are whole and complete just as you are, or calling up your well of kindness and caregiving and focusing on who needs you.

SIERRA: Whichever blessing you need is the one we hope you'll take and run with.

STEPHANIE: Because the world needs you. Not the small version of you. Not the version that fits neatly into someone else's framework.

SIERRA: The version that wanders the desert collecting bones and believes, despite all evidence to the contrary, that something alive will emerge.

STEPHANIE: We're standing at the edge with you.

SIERRA: Walk with the fear. Follow your intuition.

STEPHANIE: Or just focus on who needs what you have and let that motivation reshape you.

SIERRA: Either way, you'll get there, because you are a leader already, whether you know it or not.

ABOUT THE AUTHOR

Sierra Melcher is an award-winning, best-selling author, international speaker, and educator. She is the CEO of **Red Thread Publishing**, an independent nonfiction publishing house devoted to amplifying impactful voices.

Through Red Thread, Sierra has guided more than **400 authors from 31+ countries** to write and publish meaningful nonfiction and has overseen the publication of **75 books to date**. While the company centers and elevates women's voices, it works with authors of all genders who are committed to thoughtful leadership, integrity, and social impact.

Sierra is the author of **20 books** and holds a **Master's degree in Education**. Her work focuses on writing as a tool for leadership, legacy, and cultural change, with an emphasis on community, collaboration, and sustainable creative practice.

Originally from the United States, Sierra lives in **Medellín, Colombia**, with her daughter.

Join our community **www.skool.com/writeyourbook/about**
    www.redthreadbooks.com

ABOUT THE AUTHOR

A former U.S. Diplomat, **Stephanie Mikulasek** is Managing Director and Founder of the ServantEDGE, a company that designs and facilitates game-changing international immersion experiences, executive coaching, and experiential leadership development. Drawing from decades of global leadership, academic scholarship, and immersive transformation work, Stephanie blends wisdom, wit, and depth to inspire leaders and teams to challenge the illusion of certainty, disrupt ineffective patterns, invite radical belonging, and rediscover what matters most.

Stephanie holds a Master of Public Administration in International Management, a Master of Arts in World Religions and Cultures, and is currently a George Mason University PhD candidate researching how to develop transformational leaders through immersion experiences. She is a member of the International Coaching Federation (ICF), a certified Executive Coach from Georgetown University, and a certified Mindfulness Meditation Teacher under Jack Kornfield and Tara Brach. She has studied and trained with Dr. Richard Schwartz, Steve March, Jennifer Garvey Berger, Jim Dethmer, Kate Ebner, Humberto Maturana, and with faculty at Harvard University. She has lived, traveled, and worked in over 60 countries, and currently lives in the Pacific Northwest.

A frequent guest on podcasts, Stephanie is sought after for her engaging and dynamic keynotes and workshops. She publishes weekly on Substack and LinkedIn, and her forthcoming book is on Managing Multiple Generations in the Workplace – including AI. Connect with her on LinkedIn and at The ServantEDGE.

Chapter 2
How Resiliency Drives Purpose
—Catalina Escobar Bravo

L ong before I had language for purpose, my intuition already knew when something in my life was not moving in the right direction. On paper, things often looked right — titles, paths, expectations neatly aligned. But internally, I felt resistance. Not dramatic, not urgent. Just a quiet knowing that something was misaligned.

It took me years to understand that this discomfort was not confusion or failure. It was information; they were signals. Learning to trust those signals and act on them has been one of the hardest and most defining parts of my journey.

This is a personal story about learning to listen and to find purpose, not as a single discovery, but as an ongoing practice, and about the courage it takes to change direction when the path you are on no longer feels true.

LEARNING TO ADAPT

I was born and raised in Medellín, Colombia, at a time when both the country and the city were often described as unviable. In the 1990s, violence was not an exception; it was part of the environment. It shaped daily routines, conversations, and the way we learned to move through the world.

I encountered that reality early on. When I was nine years old, my grandfather was kidnapped. That experience exposed me to fear and uncertainty, and to the fragility of mental health, something I would only fully understand much later. As a teenager, the violence was constant: bombs, kidnappings, and killings were part of the news we consumed every day, and part of what families talked about at home.

I still remember small, concrete details that now feel surreal. We would place masking tape on the windows and sleep with them slightly open, so that if a bomb exploded nearby, the glass would not shatter and hurt us. This was not extraordinary. This was normal life.

And yet, despite all of this, I had a happy childhood and youth. That paradox has stayed with me. It taught me an early and lasting lesson about resilience, as the ability to keep living fully in imperfect and even dangerous conditions. To adapt. To find joy, connection, and meaning without denying reality.

Looking back, that context shaped who I am today and why I do what I do. It taught me about resilience and adaptation, about our capacity not only to continue thriving but also to adapt regardless of the circumstances.

This early exposure to adaptation became the foundation for many of the decisions I would later make.

NOT FITTING. THE FIRST SIGNAL

After high school, I chose to study Mechanical Engineering. People often ask me why. The honest answer is: I don't really know. I was very young and had no real tools to make such a decision. I think I wanted to do something different, something unexpected, something that challenged what was considered normal. I have always been drawn to questioning standards rather than following them.

Studying Engineering in the 1990s also meant being one of very few women in a deeply male-dominated field. That experience shaped me profoundly. I learned a lot, technically and personally, but I also became aware of the barriers women face in technical professions. Those university years were formative in many ways; they gave me lifelong friendships and helped build another pillar of who I am today.

And yet, something didn't quite fit.

I graduated into a country in crisis. Youth unemployment in Colombia rose sharply, reaching nearly 20% by the end of the decade following the 1999 financial crisis. Jobs were scarce, but my discomfort went deeper than the job market. I didn't want to work as an engineer, but I didn't know what else I wanted to do.

I remember telling a friend that I felt like a puzzle piece that didn't belong in the puzzle. Not only because I couldn't find a job, but because I couldn't find myself in the path I had chosen or in society. I had learned how to function in the system, but not how to listen to myself. I was missing something, but I didn't know what.

At the time, I experienced that feeling as confusion. Looking back, I see it for what it was: the first signal. A quiet but persistent discomfort telling me that learning and achievement were not enough, that something essential was missing. Now I know that what happened is that I hadn't found purpose yet, and my mind and intuition already knew that I was meant to look elsewhere.

LEAVING IN ORDER TO LISTEN AND CHANGE: EMIGRATING

At that point, leaving Colombia felt like the only way forward. Like many people of my generation in Colombia during the 1990s, I emigrated. In part as an escape, and in part as a search. I needed distance to find something and to find myself.

I moved to the United States, to Washington, DC, after receiving a scholarship to pursue an MBA at The George Washington University. The MBA was a bridge. A way out of engineering and into something I still couldn't name. It was also during that time that I met my husband, who, like me, was Colombian and navigating a similar sense of in-between.

Halfway through the program, the dot-com boom was at its peak.

One day, I read an article about e-business and the internet, and I felt butterflies in my stomach. Real ones. Physical. Immediate. I remember thinking: this is it. Not in a dramatic, fully formed way, but as a deep recognition and again, the intuition. Technology was giving language to something that had already been inside me: the possibility of change at scale, of systems transforming how people live, work, and connect.

From that moment on, I leaned in completely. I took every class I could on technology and digital business. I read obsessively. When I commit to something, I do it fully. After graduating, I joined a dot-com company and entered years that were fast, unstable, and profoundly formative. Companies were acquired overnight. One day we had one logo; the next day, another. I remember arriving at the office and being told to change our email signatures and manually update every document because our former employer no longer existed.

What I didn't expect was to experience not only the boom, but also the internet bubble burst.

Living through that cycle, the exhilaration, the speed, the collapse, deepened my resilience and my ability to adapt. But more importantly, it confirmed my intuition. Before my mind could fully articulate it, my body already knew where my energy belonged.

INTEGRATING PURPOSE: TECHNOLOGY + IMPACT

When it became clear that massive layoffs were coming at the dot-com company, a friend told me about an opening at the World Bank. My first reaction was confusion and disbelief. I didn't see how I would fit there, or how my background in technology and business could be useful. At that point, I knew nothing about social development. To me, social impact was something you did on the side, like volunteering or donating, not a career in itself. I genuinely didn't know you could build a professional life around impact.

I joined the World Bank to work on an initiative called the Development Gateway. Its purpose was to promote the use of the internet and technology to drive development. Suddenly, everything clicked. I worked with people from around the world, overseeing projects in Latin America and the Caribbean, and later contributed to the team that managed the Bank's intranet, creating content and digital tools for staff across the organization.

Once again, I felt that familiar sense of belonging. This was another missing piece falling into place. I realized that technology and impact were not separate paths; they were meant to be woven together. Technology was not the goal; it was the lever. Impact was not charity; it was a legitimate, demanding, and deeply strategic field where one could be successful professionally.

Those years in Washington, DC, were transformational in every sense. I got married and had my first son. In 2005, we moved to Paris, France, so my husband could pursue his MBA. I continued working remotely for the World Bank—long before remote work was normal—and our second son was born there. Eventually, we decided to return to Colombia to raise our family. The country was changing. There was a sense of possibility, of rebuilding, of the future. I had left Colombia lost and uncertain; I came back with a partner, two children, and a feeling of being on the right path.

Alongside all of this, entrepreneurship had always been quietly present. Back in university, I had started a small business with friends, making handmade jewelry to finance a trip to the United States. That impulse to create and to build has never left. During my years in Washington DC, the need to start something of my own became more insistent. So with a group of friends, we began meeting regularly, imagining what we could create once I returned to Colombia. We worked on an idea, on paper, for more than a year.

Something was already taking shape.

RETURNING TO COLOMBIA AND CREATING MAKAIA: CHOOSING TO BET

Coming back to Colombia was not a return to the same place I had left. Medellín was transforming, and I needed to understand what that transformation actually meant on the ground. While I was still consulting for the World Bank, I began visiting communities, public institutions, and potential partners; listening more than talking, trying to read and understand the city again.

We had a full-fledged business plan on paper. That was how things were done back then. I shared it with many people. The response was almost always the same: *this won't work here.* But then came the pause, and the unexpected turn: *However, given your experience, they would say, why don't you help us with this technology project in local communities?*

That was the moment where adaptation and listening mattered more than falling in love with the ideas. What we had worked on for over a year was not ready, not for this context, not for this country. But what was emerging was something more alive: the possibility of creating an organization that used technology as a tool for social development in underserved communities. Not as a theory. As practice and real change.

That is how Makaia was born. We named it Makaia which means "to build" or "to construct" in Miskito, an indigenous language from Central America, because we wanted to contribute to creating a better society.

We formally created Makaia in June 2006. At the beginning, it was just me on the ground in Colombia. My partners have always been in the United States. There was no perfect plan, no document that guided us, only momentum and conviction, teaching people technology, building capabilities, opening doors. Once again, I felt deeply aligned. This work connected my passion for technology with my commitment to social impact, entrepreneurship, and something even more personal.

Deep down, I wanted to help build a different society from the one I had grown up in. One where people had opportunities. One where violence was not the default horizon.

For a year and a half, I lived in two worlds at once. I continued consulting for the World Bank while building Makaia from scratch. At home, I had a three-year-old and a baby. I was exhausted but inspired and deeply alive. I was also confronting, again, what society expected from women: stability over risk, gratitude over ambition, safety over purpose.

Eventually, I had to choose. Either I stayed with the World Bank, or I committed fully to Makaia. For me, the decision was obvious. I felt supported by my family, but not always by society. A friend once asked me why I would dedicate my life to philanthropy, as if purpose were a waste of talent. What I was building was not fully understood. But I kept going. I trusted the vision, the mission, and the change I wanted to see. And my intuition.

Those early years at Makaia were intense, fast, and deeply fulfilling. We were growing because we were needed. Over time, Makaia became more than an idea or a project. It grew into an organization with teams, partners, and responsibilities far beyond me. It was no longer just my creation; it had become part of a broader ecosystem, serving communities, institutions, and people who depended on its continuity.

LETTING GO: THE HARDEST DECISION

By 2015, something had shifted. I didn't have the same energy to work. I was often in a bad mood, impatient, tired in a way that rest didn't fix. More than exhaustion, what I felt was disconnection. I started to sense that I was no longer being the leader Makaia needed, and that was painful to admit.

As organizations grow, leadership changes. What once required creativity, intuition, and closeness to the mission slowly turns into management, administration, and structure. That transition is necessary, but it doesn't suit everyone. In my case, the tasks that now occupied most of my time were far from the work that had originally motivated me to create Makaia. Little by little, my sense of purpose, vision, and passion began to fade.

I couldn't ignore what I was feeling. I spoke with my partners and with the board and shared what had become clear to me: Makaia needed a different type of leadership for the stage it was entering. I didn't want the title. I didn't care about the corner office or the external validation. What I wanted was to continue working with purpose, in a way that was honest, for me and for the organization.

Eventually, we agreed to bring in an external CEO. That transition was deeply personal. It required courage, resilience, and the ability to prioritize the common good over personal attachment. Over time, I learned that this kind of decision is not uncommon among entrepreneurs. Many of us are driven by the act of creating, not necessarily by managing what comes next. And recognizing where we add the most value, and where we no longer do, is also a form of leadership.

What was hardest to let go of was not the role itself, but what Makaia represented. I had created it from scratch. It felt like another baby. Letting someone else lead it meant accepting that someone could do the job better than I could, even while knowing, deep down, that I had reached my own limit as CEO. That kind of honesty is uncomfortable, especially when your identity is so closely tied to what you have built.

I also knew how this decision would be read. In many contexts, becoming CEO is seen as the pinnacle of a career. The ultimate proof of success. Walking away from that role is often interpreted as failure, weakness, or lack of ambition, particularly for women, who are still expected to hold on tightly once they "make it." I was aware of that judgment, and I felt its weight.

Letting go did not mean stepping away from purpose. It meant protecting it.

WHAT I'VE LEARNED ABOUT LEADERSHIP, RESILIENCY AND PURPOSE

What this journey has taught me is a set of lessons and a way of standing in the world.

I've learned that leadership begins with listening, deep, uncomfortable listening. Listening to context, to people, to what is actually needed, not to what we wish were true. Markets, communities, and organizations speak all the time. The challenge is to quiet our own noise long enough to hear them.

I've also learned that purpose without sustainability is fragile. Impact is not charity, and purpose-led work must be grounded in good governance and sound financial strategies. When purpose and profit are intentionally woven together, organizations become stronger, more credible, and better able to drive lasting change.

Leadership, for me, has never been about titles. It is about staying connected to the internal flame, as I call it, which is also the reason we move in the first place. That flame needs care. It needs boundaries. It takes courage to say no, to protect what matters, and sometimes to step back when your role no longer serves the mission.

One of the hardest things I've learned is that good leadership also knows when to step aside. Organizations evolve, and so must leaders. Letting go is not failure. It is one of the highest forms of responsibility. Different stages of an organization require different kinds of leadership, and honoring that truth can be an act of generosity.

I've learned that nothing meaningful is built alone. Collaboration is not a slogan or an option; it is a recognition that we are co-responsible for the societies we shape. Progress accelerates when we stop trying to carry everything ourselves, and we work with others, people and organizations.

And finally, I've learned that no leadership journey is worth it if it costs you your life outside of work. Family, relationships, health, and joy are not secondary rewards; they are the ground from which everything else grows.

To the women who are already leading and quietly doubting the path you are on: you are not broken for feeling the need to change. Listening to that voice does not make you weak; it makes you honest.

To the younger women: you don't need to have it all figured out. You only need to pay attention to what feels alive, and to trust yourself enough to move when it's time. Look for your internal flame, the signals that make you feel alive and energized. That is not a distraction. That is information. And that is often where your next step begins.

ABOUT OF AUTHOR

Catalina Escobar Bravo works at the intersection of technology, international development, and social change. For more than 25 years, she's built and led initiatives that use technology to expand access to opportunity — particularly in education and the future of work. CoFounder at Makaia (www.makaia.org), BeTek (www.betek.la) and Nodoká (www.nodoka.co).

She's a founder, board member, and lifelong learner; born and raised in Colombia, attended grad school in the United States, and shaped by global experience. Mechanical engineer, MBA. Mother of two young men.

www.linkedin.com/in/catalinaescobarbravo

Chapter 3
Despite The Fear
—Carol Britton

When I reflect on my career spanning over 30 years in the business world, I realize that many things that seemed crucial at the time were actually insignificant. Landing my dream job was an exception; the feelings of importance, excitement, and fear are still with me today. I was determined to use these feelings, especially the fear, to propel me forward, not stop me dead in my tracks. Early in my career, I let fear overcome my confidence, and it stopped me from speaking up, thus holding me back when I should have been moving forward.

My family and I had relocated several times, primarily for my husband's career. At one point, we moved to Alabama for my job. While my husband, a native Southerner, loved living there, I faced challenges in the workplace. Being labeled a "female Yankee" added an extra layer of difficulty to my professional role. To overcome these feelings of inadequacy, I found myself trying to overperform by embracing my "female Yankee" identity, which did not go well in a southern, male-dominated environment. So, when the opportunity for me to land a position with a large, global financial services company came up, I was excited.

I was concerned about how this would impact my husband. He was always supportive of my career, but this would require us to move to New York City, a city I knew my husband would rather not live in. When we discussed it, he encouraged me to interview, but I knew deep down he did not want to leave Alabama. My husband was Vice President of Sales, so he could work from anywhere, but he loved living in the South. For me to move forward with the interview process, this would truly have to be my dream job.

I decided to proceed with the interviews for the Chief Procurement Officer (CPO) role at the Bank of New York in New York City. At the very least, it would give me a chance to brush up on my interviewing skills. The initial interview was with the recruiter via video in a studio designed for this style of interview. I always felt I presented myself better in person. Entering a room, standing up straight, offering a strong handshake, and looking someone in the eye is much different than sitting in front of a camera. I won't lie - under the bright lights, my nerves were on edge, and I could feel myself sweating under my suit coat. I tamped down my nerves and fears and put my best foot forward. Afterall, I was gainfully employed and didn't need this job (but I wanted it!). The conversation went well, the recruiter was easy to talk to, and the conversation flowed. I effectively communicated how my experience aligned with the organization's needs and that I would be an asset to the team. After overcoming the nerves of my initial interview, I felt a sense of accomplishment. However, this was just the beginning, and the thought of moving to New York City presented its own set of challenges.

When I received the call to continue in the interview process, I was thrilled. Then I was told I would have to fly to New York City for the next round of interviews. I was "excitified" – excited and terrified at the same time. I was excited to go on to the next round of interviews, but terrified about going to New York, navigating the city, and crushing the interviews. Not to mention, the interviews were being conducted at the company's headquarters located at One Wall Street. I was intimidated by the address, but knew I was going to impress the people who worked there. I had to face my fears again and give myself a pep talk. With leadership experience in automotive, manufacturing, and financial services, I knew I was more than qualified for the job. I had the experience and qualifications that the company needed to make the required changes, and I wanted it.

The interviews went well, and I felt confident about receiving an offer. However, the prospect of getting the job scared me more than the possibility of not getting it. *Could I keep up the pace? Would I be able to navigate the city's complex transportation system?* Most of all, I was terrified of failing in such a high-stakes role. The song lyrics from "New York, New York" - "And if I can make it there, I'm gonna make it anywhere, it's up to you, New York, New York"- was an earworm I couldn't get rid of. At times, it elated me, and at others, it reminded me of what was at stake.

The recruiter I was working with provided a lot of insight into the company, which was reinforced by what I read in the annual report and listened to on the quarterly earnings call. In the annual report, the Bank referenced that expenses were not in alignment, hence a focus on cost reduction. During the quarterly earnings call, the president of the bank said that the Procurement function was underperforming, and there was a heightened focus on improving it. A company that publicly states they are focused on expense control and improving the procurement function told me it was very serious about achieving this objective. Knowing that my success or failure would be publicly available on the quarterly earnings calls and closely watched by Wall Street analysts, the CFO and CEO had me terrified.

As I was interviewing for the CPO role, I asked the following questions: "What is your perception of the current Procurement function and why? What do you see as the biggest challenge for Procurement? What is one thing you'd change, if you were me, on Day One? What is one thing Procurement does well?" The responses I received were consistent and difficult to hear. Procurement was described as a "bureaucratic bottleneck, painfully slow, no value add, roadblock" – well, you get the picture. I realized that if I received and accepted an offer, I would be stepping into a position that was not well-received across the organization.

Understanding that I was joining an organization where the

Procurement function was held in low regard and publicly acknowledged as underperforming, I knew that significant changes were necessary. These changes were going to have to be done well, but in a manner that enabled lasting change. When I received the job offer, I knew I would have to use fear to propel me forward, not stop me dead in my tracks. It would require me to conduct a holistic review, break tasks down into manageable steps, and use my experience and expertise to accomplish each task. I had to use my first fifteen days on the job to analyze the data and develop a semblance of a plan. This included the information from the interviews, talent and process reviews, and spend data. The next fifteen days would be used to validate the information and gain buy-in from the key stakeholders. Gathering the inputs in the first thirty days was crucial to the execution of my 100-day plan.

When I started with the Bank of New York, one of the first things I did was to read annual performance reviews for my entire team. I was expecting to see the typical bell curve of reviews with the majority in the "meets expectations" range. I anticipated there may be a bit of a heavier group in the "unacceptable and room for improvement" categories, given the remarks about Procurement being in the bottom quartile.

I read the first dozen reviews and was amazed that they were all rated "exceeds expectations" or "above average." So, I skipped straight to the rating section of the next dozen reviews and found the same thing. How could this be if the Procurement team was viewed so poorly by the rest of the organization? To find out, I went straight to the source.

I conducted one-on-one meetings with my direct reports, and their direct reports helped me understand their management styles and rapport with their respective teams. What I found out through these conversations was very enlightening. It was rumored that a rating of "meets expectations" was not acceptable, so the truly high performers were rated "exceeds expectations," and everyone else was rated "above average." Ah ha! With the team members receiving glowing reviews, they thought they were performing well, and there was no need for them to change how they conducted business. I needed to talk to Human Resources immediately to start a full review process of the team and begin rebuilding. I also spoke with my manager, letting him know this process would start immediately and I would need his backing and support to hire the right talent and, unfortunately, lay off those that didn't have the skill set to move procurement to the upper quartile. I was very fearful of this process. I knew it meant I would be impacting people's livelihoods, some in a negative manner and others in a positive way. The importance of having a solid team was essential to the overall success of my plan, and I knew it would require the most focus. I kept the renowned business author Jim Collins' quote about talent, from "Good to Great" in the forefront of my mind: "First get the right people on the bus, then get the wrong people off the bus, and finally get the right people in the right seats, and then you figure out where to drive the bus." This reminded me I had to focus on getting the right people onboard before I could finalize and begin execution of the strategy. I knew when I accepted the offer that the biggest and hardest changes would be related to the talent. I never lost sight of the impact this would have on people. I had to face my fear and do the right thing for the people who would be retained and the people who would be let go. While not easy, working with the Human Resources team and with management support, we worked through the process as seamlessly as possible. Some members of my inherited team had spent their entire careers at the Bank of New York. This is both good and bad. They knew the organization and the culture very well, but they were set in the way things operated, so change might be very hard for them.

To analyze the data and create a comprehensive go-forward plan, I would need help I didn't have inside the organization. The plan had to have three primary areas of focus: people, processes, and technology. While I would have liked the luxury of conducting these focus areas as three distinct areas, the fact that they impacted each other meant I had to tackle them all at once.

Knowing I didn't have the right talent "on the bus," I approached my manager, the CFO, to ask for outside help. I needed help analyzing the talent, the spend data, and the processes. As he was the CFO, the numbers would have to make sense. Also, the timeline and key milestones needed to be detailed so there would be a clear manner to track progress.

It's important to note that within my first few days on the job, my finance partner and I met. She provided me with a savings target, and I was shocked by how low the number was. She informed me that the company had used a benchmarking firm to review the spend data and provide a target. The number the benchmarking firm provided was 3% of the addressable spend. Addressable spend is not the total expenses of the company; it is only the portion of the spend that the procurement department can actually influence or negotiate. For example, it does not include items such as payroll and taxes.

Based on my experience, savings on addressable spend typically averaged around 10%. Therefore, I was shocked by the 3% target, particularly given the procurement function's bottom-quartile status. Fear crept back in at this point. What was I missing? How could an outside firm analyze the spend and come back with only a 3% savings target? I had a choice to make. I could simply accept the 3% target and move on, or I could conduct my own analysis and redefine the target. I chose the latter. I knew this was a risk; if my suspicions were correct, the reward would be tremendous.

The consulting firm I wanted to hire was willing to conduct the data analysis at no cost, even if they weren't hired, because they also felt the initial savings target was too low. This would make the discussion I needed to have with my manager easier. If the numbers revealed what I thought they would, I would need to hire the consulting firm immediately. This was all happening within the first few weeks, and I only had one shot at getting it right. My fear that I was right about the numbers and needed to change the target created more fear because the numbers would have to be met or exceeded – no excuses.

One of the methods I use to manage fear and anxiety is to run. I'm a long-distance runner, which helps me process and think through issues while I run. During this period, I spent my mornings running along the West Side Highway or on a treadmill, going through the plan, rehearsing my pitch, and formulating answers to the questions I thought my manager might have. This was time well spent not only for me physically, but mentally as well. I've always used running as a time to process things going on in my life, and it remains one of my most valuable tools to this day.

When I met with my manager, I was confident in the plan. The data I gathered enabled me to map out my first 100 days with clarity and be prepared for his questions. However, I knew this was my make-or-break moment, and I couldn't screw it up. So, I wasn't "excitified" for this meeting; I was just flat out terrified.

I would like to say it was easier than I thought it would be to align my manager with the 100-day plan, but it wasn't. He understood the need to conduct a full talent review and supported the necessary changes. However, when it came to changing the savings target, he challenged me. He needed to make sure that increasing the target by more than 3-fold was realistic. This was a huge number, and if the target was changed, it would have to be met. I was prepared for this by taking the time to anticipate what drives a CFO. I had examples of where the savings opportunities were and how they would be addressed. For example, office supplies were out of control. Most companies have a very limited list of office supplies that an employee can purchase. When reviewing office supply spend, I found that any employee could purchase any office supplies from the full catalog provided by the office supply company. The fact that the company purchased over 200 types of file folders in one year was a very impactful example to show my manager. If "simple" spend controls were not in place, then the ability to impact meaningful expense reductions across the company was very realistic. The other challenge was tracking the savings to make sure they hit the bottom line of the company. Before this meeting, my finance partner and I agreed that finance, not procurement, would track the savings through the budget and report quarterly on the actual savings vs the projected targets. This would provide visibility and accountability across the organization, and my manager was pleased with this methodology.

The months that followed were some of the longest and hardest in my career, but the work paid off. The necessary changes to talent and required skill sets went as well as could be expected, but gave me heartburn every single day. During this time, I spent as much time as possible running outside to keep myself focused and sane! The savings targets were exceeded, but some of the expense reductions did not make me a very popular person in the company. For example, when reducing the variety of office supplies, I took a lot of heat for eliminating certain types of file folders. I knew this would be the case, but I couldn't let the fear of being disliked overpower my ability to execute the strategy. By facing my fear of failure, I was able to make it in New York. It enabled me to make a smooth transition with my family to New York City and provided the motivation and clarity needed to move forward.

Moving to New York City and taking on the role of Chief Procurement Officer at the Bank of New York was daunting, but it taught me invaluable lessons about resilience, determination, and the importance of having a supportive network. I earned several promotions during my tenure at the Bank; each one was scary. Despite the fear each promotion created, it provided the momentum to move forward. The last role I held was Chief Operating Officer - Corporate Services, where I managed a team of over 1,000 employees and contractors. Facing my fears contributed to my success by enabling me to face challenges head-on rather than avoiding them.

My story is a testament to the power of determination and the belief that, despite the fear, you can achieve great things.

To those reading this chapter, remember that fear is a natural part of any significant change. Embrace it, use it as a driving force, and never let it hold you back. You are stronger than you think, and the greatest moments of your life often lie just beyond your comfort zone.

ABOUT THE AUTHOR

Carol Britton, as a collaborator with vast experience and through sound strategy development, has driven efficiencies across the organizations she has been affiliated with. She has streamlined diverse operations and processes, delivering notable impacts to the bottom line. Carol is an inspirational leader who values both her success and the success of everyone on the teams she builds equally. Admired by her peers, team members, and other senior leaders, she is recognized for her aptitude to take complex information and distill it into an efficient and effective plan of action. Throughout her career, she has demonstrated resilience and determination, overcoming numerous challenges to achieve her goals. Her journey has taken her through various roles and relocations, including a significant position as the Chief Procurement Officer at the Bank of New York. Carol's experiences have taught her the importance of having a supportive network and the power of determination in achieving great things.

www.linkedin.com/in/carol-britton-47a2257

www.instagram.com/cabritton441

www.facebook.com/carol.britton.355

Chapter 4
A Spider Web in a Storm
—Anna Dravland

Editor's Note: *Some stories do not follow a straight line. They arrive in fragments: moments, memories, and sensations that resist tidy arcs or easy lessons. They mirror how life is actually lived: nonlinear, embodied, and sometimes unresolved.*

Anna's chapter is offered in this spirit.

Following a severe brain injury and stroke, writing in a traditional, linear structure is not possible for her. The form of this chapter reflects how she now communicates and organizes experience. In honoring her voice, we chose not to reshape the story to fit conventional expectations, but to protect the authenticity of how it was shared.

At Red Thread Publishing, we believe leadership stories do not need to conform to inherited structures to be powerful or true. Femme Led was created to expand what leadership looks like and sounds like, especially in women's voices.

As you read, we invite you to listen for resonance. Leadership is not always neat, and becoming is rarely chronological for any of us.

*— **Sierra Melcher***

Editor & Publisher, Red Thread Publishing

BUILDING A SPIDERWEB IN A STORM

Trying to keep my nonprofit alive through everything that happened to my brain & body has felt like building a spiderweb in the middle of a storm.

Each time the wind ripped through it, I started again.

Each time the rain washed it away, I adapted.

Each time I lost strength, memory, or fought for my life — I found a new way to pivot instead of quit.

I had launched 'Spread Goodness Day' just three weeks before my health began to collapse under the force of a massive stroke. Three weeks. That's how close hope and devastation lived to one another in my story. While the vision was still in its infancy, my body was already beginning to fail me.

And the leader I had always been — the woman who could do it all, be everywhere, talk to everyone, carry the load — disappeared overnight.

Suddenly, I became the woman who could do almost nothing at all.

I could no longer rely on the abilities that had once defined me: my memory, my energy, my mobility, my sharpness. Leadership, as I had known it, was gone. In its place was confusion, exhaustion, cognitive loss, and the slow, terrifying realization that the body I had led with could no longer keep up with the mind that dreamed everything into existence.

I had to become a completely different kind of leader.

Not the one who did everything…

But the one who learned how to ask for everything.

Spread Goodness Day was kept alive by phone calls I barely had the strength to complete.

By volunteers who became my hands when mine wouldn't work.

By voices that carried the vision when I couldn't speak clearly.

By people who believed in the mission even when I couldn't recognize the woman who created it.

Leadership became collaboration.

Strength became surrender.

Power became vulnerability.

There is nothing glamorous about that kind of transformation. It strips you of ego, of pride, of the identity you once used to survive in the world.

Letting go of who I was so I could survive as who I was becoming was the most painful leadership lesson I have ever learned.

But also the most sacred.

Because, slowly, I realized something else was happening:

The mission was no longer built on my individual capacity alone — it was being built on community.

And that is the truest form of leadership there is.

In losing my ability to do everything, I created space for others to step in.

In releasing control, I created belonging.

In surrendering the image of "strong," I created something much stronger than myself.

And somehow — against every medical prediction, cognitive limitation, and physical barrier — Spread Goodness Day kept going.

Not because I was powerful.

But because goodness is.

As long as we keep the strength to ask for help. To let ourselves have limits— there is no storm that can fully tear down what was meant to change the world. Because it doesn't just belong to me anymore. It belongs to all of us.

BREAKING THE "STRONG WOMAN" MYTH: CHOOSING HELP, HOPE, AND HUMILITY

True leadership isn't self-sacrifice — it's the courage to be supported.

My life has systematically dismantled the idea that strong women must do everything alone. I survived a stroke, medical anorexia, severe complications, trauma, addiction, homelessness, and the loss of my career — and yet continued with the non-profit Spread Goodness Day. With help, I was able to curate a statewide, multi-state movement founded on goodness.

Not because I "powered through," but because I finally allowed myself to accept help: medical help, emotional help, community support, and the kindness of strangers and friends.

The strongest man or woman, under the pressure of the heaviest weight they can hold up, is using every…single…ounce…of what they carry for MOMENTS. Knees buckling, arms shaking. Veins bulging, blood vessels bursting. We are not meant to bear that weight for hours, days, years…a lifetime. Can we expect someone to be so strong every day and moment?

It has taken me years to let go of the pressure to be unshakable. To hold the weight and never drop it. Overcoming an entire lifetime of hyper productivity and the "if you want it done right; do it myself mindset."

But, after my stroke, pushing for that kind of strength nearly destroyed me. But the more I refused help, the more it delayed healing and the success of my nonprofit organization. That even now, I struggle with feeling weak because I can't do things the way other people do. I have to cut corners, cancel meetings. Can't go to events. I'm completely unreliable. My energy and health can have me going for a hike one day and unable to make a sandwich the next.

Asking for help became the only way I could be a leader of anything. Often asking other people to lead things for me. Making sure that my website has free tools and ways for people to celebrate and spread goodness without ever speaking with me. Leadership became building my life like a starfish instead of a spider web. When you cut off the leg of a starfish, everything keeps functioning until that limb can re-heal. I needed to build something that functioned without me. Moved without me.

I want my experiences to give women permission not to crumble. To rest and rebuild. To ask for what you need to be successful. Whether it as a mom, a business owner, a coworker or a nonprofit leader — asking for help has been one of the most empowering things I've ever learned. Commitment to my mission and surrendering to the support of others. Functioning with I have. It required a level of emotional honesty that exposed a vulnerability that's hard to describe. I am still fighting the feeling of shame when I make a phone call asking somebody for support. To give their energy to my mission. Sometimes I still don't make that phone call and ask. But every time someone takes my invitation to help change the world, whether it be through advocacy or spreading goodness, I feel stronger. Because I'm not bearing all the weight in the world alone. Because I don't have to rebuild my web in every storm. I became a starfish and instead of a spider. And I learned to build everything else in my event and nonprofit so it lives every day without me.

I hope this resonates deeply with women founders, executives, and leaders who feel pressured to remain invincible. To keep carrying that weight and never drop it. To keep rebuilding everything in the middle of lifes storms.

ABOUT THE AUTHOR

Anna Dravland is a proud alumna of Northern Michigan University, where her passion for service, event planning, and community impact first took root. She is the founder of Spread Goodness Day, an nationally recognized holiday celebrated annually on the second Friday of March, inspiring individuals, schools, and organizations to create an explosive atmosphere of empowerment that we can change the world every day. After surviving a massive stroke in 2017 and navigating complex ongoing health challenges, Anna describes herself as medically retired against her will. Her journey has deepened her commitment to advocacy, resilience, and proving that purpose is not limited by circumstance.

www.facebook.com/spreadgoodnessday
www.instagram.com/spreadgoodnessday
www.tiktok.com/@spreadgoodnessday
www.instagram.com/survivingwithgoodness

Chapter 5
Becoming Brave
A Southern Woman's Journey of Reinvention, Resilience, and Courageous Leadership
—Tracy Macdonald

Twelve years ago, as a diplomatic spouse, I stepped off a plane into a remote country. In college, I had studied in Europe, and early in my banking career, I'd worked in London, but this was different. The air was thick with heat, swirling with intoxicating scents, and I was surrounded by distinct clicking sounds of the local SiSwati language. My entire world had shifted overnight– it was exhilarating, yet terrifying.

The next morning, my husband Brad left early for his job at the U.S. Embassy, and I stood holding Ramsay, our infant son, feeling lost in the barren home that had been assigned to us for the next three years. The perimeter of our yard was secured by high walls topped with coils of barbed wire, and I jumped when a roving guard passed the living room window, which was decorated with wrought-iron bars.

To follow Brad's career overseas, I'd left my consulting practice behind and was now unemployed at age 41 for the first time in *twenty* years. I was quietly envious that Brad was going to work and had colleagues to talk to. It was only 6:45 a.m.–the start of a long day without much structure, which did not suit my Type A personality.

Slowly, I began unpacking our suitcases, wondering how to rebuild our life in Swaziland* when everything was unfamiliar and had far fewer resources than we were accustomed to. Our household effects and car wouldn't arrive by cargo ship for months. How could I get out to buy groceries? Was it safe to explore on foot beyond our walls? How would I navigate the maze of dirt roads and find places for my child to play, or for me to find friends? Who was I without my job, daily routines, and my community? And what were my hobbies? It had been decades since I'd had this kind of free time.

In the midst of overwhelm and uncertainty, a calm voice inside said: *You will figure this out.* That moment was one of several that reinforced this truth: growth and leadership are not built in clarity. They are built in uncertainty—and refined by the choices we make when we feel unsteady. This revelation has shaped my entire leadership philosophy: growth doesn't wait for your readiness. It demands that you trust yourself long before you feel certain.

This chapter is not simply the story of my career. It is the journey of how a young woman, who doubted her strength, became more fully herself and a leader by trusting her voice. It is a roadmap for professional women navigating transition, reinvention, and purpose, in a world that doesn't always expect us to lead—but desperately needs us to.

The wise poet Adrienne Rich says, "The most important thing one woman can do for another is to illumine and expand her sense of possibilities." I hope by sharing some of my professional and personal stories that I can do that for you. I'm proof that you can thrive amidst chaos, and I'll impart wisdom I've learned from years as a female professional in male-dominated fields, and as someone who has reinvented herself several times, across continents, navigating situations that called for courage, resilience, and a new definition of self-worth.

Sitting in a college French class more than twenty-five years ago, I never would have guessed that one day I'd be using those language skills as a Federal Agent, translating for the Director of the Secret Service at a G-8 Summit dinner, then protecting Jacques Chirac, the former President of France. Or that I'd rely on French daily in Gabon years later to succeed in diplomatic life. I say this not to boast, but to illustrate that none of this could I have predicted or planned. You never know where your skills will take you, especially if you're willing to take healthy risks and stretch beyond your comfort zone.

I was never the woman who "always knew" what she wanted. However, in college, I was serious about getting good grades and ambitious about identifying a career path. In four years, I spent three semesters abroad and changed my major three times. I started out wanting to be a psychologist, but when exposed to recorded therapy sessions (with the client names redacted), I sobbed through all of them. I was too sensitive, unable to distance myself from their pain.

As a teen, I had seen the classic movie *The Silence of the Lambs*, one of the first films to portray a female agent on the big screen. Jody Foster starred as FBI Agent Clarice Starling, and I wanted to be her. In college, when a pregnant female Georgia Bureau of Investigation (GBI) agent visited my abnormal psychology class and shared about her life in criminal behavior and forensics, I was convinced she had the job I wanted. However, after looking into an internship, I couldn't stomach the crime scene photos. So, as graduation closed in, I changed my major yet again and left college with a freshly minted B.A. in Sociology, with too fragile a heart to pursue social work and without a clue how to find a job in my field.

After graduation, I returned to my hometown and was recruited into a new credit card processing company that was hiring corporate trainers to teach bank software. Not only did that sound boring and dry, but I knew nothing about computer data or bank transactions. However, the paycheck was attractive, so I said yes and began flailing my way through the anti-fraud software.

Initially, I wasn't confident and didn't understand all of the analytics, but I practiced persistence. I showed up in the face of uncertainty, asked frequent questions, and studied the patterns in the transaction details. Those skills, though I didn't recognize them at the time, would become the backbone of my leadership identity: curiosity, analysis, determination, and a willingness to learn (and admit) what I did not know.

A year after being hired, thanks to my French skills, I visited banks in France with senior leadership to deliver fraud detection presentations. One thing led to another, and I moved abroad as one of the company's youngest expats in sales. I loved every minute of my three years in London, traveling around to banks across Europe.

When 9/11 happened, hijackers had used a Bank of America credit card to pay for Cessna flying lessons, among other purchases. At work, I was summoned to a meeting with the United States Secret Service (USSS) to show them the credit card transaction locations, times, and date stamps to assist with finding security footage.

I'd always assumed USSS agents just protected the President. When I learned their mission also involved working on counterfeit and financial crime investigations—an area I already excelled in (and generally without any violence)– I felt a spark that surprised me. It wasn't ego. It was alignment.

At the time, the Secret Service was only 10% women, and they were seeking recruits with financial backgrounds and with a foreign language. I didn't feel ready. I didn't feel strong enough. But I said yes anyway, launching my non-linear, non-traditional career path into mostly male-dominated fields in law enforcement, then later in the intelligence community and as an instructor for the Department of Defense, teaching illicit finance to soldiers.

It was at the Federal Law Enforcement Training Center as a Secret Service recruit that I learned what I was truly capable of– how mentally tough I could be. The odds were stacked against me: I was a petite, people-pleasing, southern female bank analyst, surrounded by former Marines and police officers who already possessed much of the training I'd need to learn from scratch.

The first week of defensive tactics, my instructor—an ex-Marine— told me to stand on a yellow star in the mat room.

"Ever had your southern belle rung?" he asked.

I shook my head.

"You'll get hit so you'll know how it feels, survive the shock, and get back up. Don't move, understand?" he barked.

I tensed as his boxing glove came at me full force. I woke up on the floor to the smell of the sweaty mat beneath me, with ringing in my ears, a splitting ache behind my upper cheekbone, and a new understanding of my own limits. When I was instructed to quickly grab water in the hall, I still remember bending over that water fountain with my tears and blood dripping onto it, silently pleading with the universe for an excuse not to return to the mat room. I found my composure, but in the barracks that night, holding a bag of frozen peas against my shiner, I seriously considered quitting. Growing up, I was a swimmer and a dancer. I'd never been hit, which was a blessing, but that punch underscored just how unprepared I was for the paramilitary challenges ahead.

I called a trusted friend, a graduate from the U.S. Military Academy at West Point, who advised, "You know what they told us at the Academy? Quit tomorrow. Then make sure tomorrow never comes until graduation day." I took his words to heart, relying on them to power through my training. I returned the next day. And the next. There were days when my mantra was: *just make it meal to meal*. I would rise, go to breakfast, then convince myself to get to lunch. At lunch, I would focus on making it to dinner. In between, I mastered firearms, passed legal exams, honed my situational awareness skills, and learned to run faster and fight back harder. Along the way, I also built endurance I didn't know my body could carry while exerting calm under pressure.

The day I walked across that stage to graduate, I was one of three women out of 24 recruits who had successfully made it through training. I was incredibly proud to receive those credentials; that badge was worth every hurdle. Hear me when I say that ***you are stronger than you think***, truly.

Now, to a few lessons I wish I'd known sooner…

EMBRACE THE FEMININE AND SET BOUNDARIES

As an agent at the field office, there were additional challenges. There were few female comrades with whom to commiserate or get advice from, and if I'm honest, I had an identity crisis. Surrounded by men, I'd put on invisible armor along with my weapon and march around, acting more masculine than I felt.

During the day, I was either armed in a dark suit for protection assignments or in combat gear to conduct raids and execute arrests. Yet in my free time, I was in sundresses and makeup. It made me feel like two separate people, incongruous. But it turns out you *can* be both–strong and soft, allowing yourself to embrace the feminine while also carrying out tasks more commonly associated with men.

It wasn't an easy path to feminine power, however. Although I carried my credentials and handcuffs (and my SIG Sauer 357) just like the male agents, at every turn, I felt I had to prove myself above and beyond to deflect the comments that "I wasn't tough enough, mean enough, strong enough,..." But, ultimately? –I started to see my unique value. I got just as many arrests as they did. Criminals underestimated me. Colleagues overlooked me—until my investigations produced results they couldn't ignore. Perpetrators confessed things to me they likely wouldn't have told a male agent, and I could read emotional nuance that was invisible to others. When criminals didn't detect that I was a police officer during undercover operations, it helped my whole squad.

My Special Agent in Charge told me that even though I wasn't as rough as the other agents, I was "a flower amongst the weeds," and that he was proud to have me on his team. His words were validating. I learned it was okay to be myself, be vulnerable, and do things my own way. Working in a male-dominated field forced me to examine the parts of myself I had once thought made me weaker or "less than"–my empathy, intuition, diplomacy, and tendency to observe before speaking. Ultimately, these traits became my competitive advantage.

Every time you show up in life, you bring an asset to the table–your unique feminine perspective. More than our male counterparts, we tend to ask for permission and hesitate to share our ideas. I encourage you to shift that mindset. Show up, find your voice, and take up space because *you deserve to be here.*

One of my greatest lessons was learning that boundaries are a form of self-respect. Raised to be a people-pleaser, it took me years of practice to not martyr myself, prioritizing the comfort of others at my own expense. I was afraid to say NO and hurt others' feelings, or to be perceived as someone who wasn't a team player. Please don't value others' feelings above your own–it's not fair to you. Protect your time, energy, and heart.

As exceptional women, you will have many demands pulling you in different directions. As leaders, others will ask a lot of you and have high expectations. Say yes only if it's an all-encompassing yes, and get comfortable saying no.

TURN FEAR INTO FUEL AND TUNE OUT THE CRITICS

Don't avoid discomfort by staying inside what feels safe and familiar. Like exercising a muscle, putting yourself in challenging situations becomes easier the more you do it. Likely, anytime you're out there taking healthy risks, you will not feel ready. I encourage you to do it anyway, push away the negative self-talk, doubts, naysayers, and the "mind monkeys" that creep in when you're scared. Instead, focus on the milestones that you've already achieved to remind you that you are solidly capable. And use that fear as a positive sign of growth. Anything new can be scary, but remember that most of the time, on the other side of fear is something fabulous, and if you don't try, you won't know–don't deny yourself the chance to find out!

Every step of becoming an agent–including the application process–I had to stay determined to ignore the criticism. Getting through the physical part of the Federal Law Enforcement Center was one of my life's most difficult challenges, and the old boy's network was in full force.

I took a 50% pay cut to work for the federal government. People said I was crazy, that I was taking a huge career step backwards from banking. It was a constant battle to quiet my doubts and turn my fear into the fire and fuel that propelled me forward. Instead of being a proud trailblazer for other female agents, I often felt like an imposter. But at the Atlanta field office, where I lacked experience in the field, I learned to make up for it as a sharp investigator, relying on my financial analysis skills.

Imposter syndrome is real. There have been many times in my life when my achievements felt like I'd just gotten lucky. But that's not true– it wasn't luck. It was persistence in facing my fears and focusing instead on being driven to learn whatever I needed to in order to succeed.

In my early 30's, working as a consultant on my first federal government contract, I was given instructions laden with an alphabet soup of military acronyms, then told to report to "the Scud missile at 0800 on Bolling Air Force Base." I humbly admit, I had to go home and Google an image of what a Scud missile looked like. (It turns out you can't miss it– it's like a small version of the Space Shuttle). There will be times like that, when you are overwhelmed and unsure of the next right step, but just show up anyway. Just write it down, look it up, and figure it out, one step at a time.

When you simply don't feel confident or up to the task, reflect on your past accomplishments to shift perspective. One memorable day, I was headed to a meeting with an Army general to give an asymmetrical warfare brief. I was running late, very pregnant, and riddled with nerves. On the highway, sitting in traffic, my car inched past the Pentagon on my left, and a realization hit me. I said aloud to myself, "You know what? I'm driving to a job where I fight terrorism, and according to my OBGYN, I am also growing eyelashes on this baby today. Top *that,* fellas!" Sometimes, it just takes reframing the fear to adopt a warrior mindset.

WHEN YOUR FOUNDATION SHIFTS, IT'S OKAY TO PIVOT

High achievers can be so focused on a goal that they forget to stop and ask themselves whether that goal still aligns with their purpose and desires. You may wake up and realize you've climbed the wrong corporate ladder, or that you're following someone else's dream. Or, in my case, perhaps it's not the dream you thought it would be. And, because you're like me–driven and ambitious– you're likely to beat yourself up when you realize you've made a mistake. But try not to. You are a human *being*, not a human *doing,* and it will work out. These experiences and lessons will serve you well later.

After jostling like an ill-fitting puzzle piece for years, I've learned that instead of trying to stay the course when something (or someone) no longer aligns, or trying to fit in when it no longer suits you, it's much better to focus on what sets you apart, your unique contribution to the world, and to honor the changes you need to make as you evolve.

Being a federal agent was exhilarating—but also morally complex. My first arrest involved separating a family, leaving a four-year-old boy to enter the foster system. Another case involved a man who had embezzled funds to pay for his wife's terminal illness treatments. I was running on fast food, with little sleep for months at a time, and felt the weight of every decision. I started asking myself deeper questions:

Is the work I'm doing aligned with my values?

Can I carry the weight of my actions long term?

What kind of leader am I becoming?

When I got brutally honest with myself and admitted that the Secret Service was no longer a good fit for me, I initially felt guilt and shame for "giving up," and concerned that I'd misled the community and family who had rallied behind my success.

Leaving federal service took more strength than joining it. The day I turned in my badge and weapon, I felt defeated because I could no longer sustain the physical and emotional tolls the job required. But, in time, I realized it took enormous courage to honor my truth and change course.

It's okay to pivot, to change your mind, and to reinvent yourself. The skills you're acquiring now, even if they seem random, are never wasted. We're all just adding tools to the toolbox on this journey of growth.

My professional life took a winding path, an interesting one that I couldn't predict and wouldn't change. I still became an agent–against the odds. No one can take that achievement away from me, nor the leadership insights I gained along the way–especially how to redefine success and embrace self-worth that's not reliant on a paycheck, others' opinions, or sources outside of myself.

CULTIVATE COURAGE AND BUILD RESILIENCE

After leaving the Secret Service, I transitioned into intelligence work in Washington, D.C. Then, after years of consulting, married a diplomat and moved overseas. The world became my classroom, and *reinvention became my new lifestyle*. Every couple of years, we uprooted our lives —new countries, new cultures, new risks, and new roles.

We've lived in East Africa, Cairo, Honduras, and West Central Africa– places considered to be hardship tours, meaning they are nations experiencing higher threat levels at the time of posting. (For example, spikes in crime, political instability, food scarcity, or lack of American-standard resources such as education and medical care). When we were posted in Cairo (now deemed safe), there were bombings against Coptic Christians and retaliations from the Muslim Brotherhood against the presidency. In Honduras, we experienced gang warfare and violent protests, and more recently, in Gabon, there was a political uprising.

Yes, there are occasional red-carpet parties, and the majority of the time, our life abroad sings to my nomadic heart. I meet fascinating people and explore off-the-grid places that satiate my wanderlust and desire for adventure. I'm a huge proponent for traveling, studying abroad, and getting outside of your comfort zone and our borders. You will gain a deeper understanding and appreciation of the United States by being outside of it–seeing other countries, learning other cultures, and witnessing that many others do not have the rights, resources, and freedoms that we have.

However, life as an expat can entail a lot more *grit* than glamour. Imagine this happening: two years ago, it was the day before my 11-year-old son and I were due to fly from Atlanta, Georgia, back to Gabon for the start of 6th grade. We went to sleep, then the phone rang in the middle of the night. It was a robotic call from the State

Department asking me to simply "Press 1 if you are safe." It was an accountability phone tree that had been activated, which meant something had gone horribly wrong at the U.S. Embassy in Libreville, where my husband was head of security.

I later discovered there had been a military coup, an arrest of the sitting Gabonese President. Consequently, my son's international school collapsed financially, and we had to send him to boarding school, turning our lives upside down while our family scrambled to adjust.

My only child wasn't supposed to leave the nest until college. It took months for our family to adapt to this unexpected, heart-wrenching dynamic. I turned to my leadership skills to get through it: show up, face the fears, and keep moving forward. I looked for the lessons and relied on what grounds me: (yoga, nature walks, morning routines, journaling, and abundance mindset practices). That year apart, I spent our savings flying back and forth for boarding school visits, guilty for leaving my husband behind in West Africa for long stretches during tumult, then torn up for leaving my young son at school for months at a time.

I frequently reminded myself that I did not have to pretend that everything was okay. I allowed myself to be vulnerable, letting the tears from mommy guilt and homesickness for my child flow across the phone lines with trusted friends, while also cultivating courage, one step at a time. And I frequently reminded myself of what I'd gotten through in the past–and come out on the other side– alive and *stronger*.

As a family, we made the sacrifice together and got through it. When our expat, nomadic lifestyle feels heaviest, we've learned to shift perspective by focusing on the positive moments, the ones where we think, "oh my gosh, pinch me– we are so fortunate for these amazing experiences–" because we *are*. We've chosen this Foreign Service path, and find the rewards greater than the hardships, which is why we continue to do it.

Of course, there are still tough times. Like when we return to the U.S. on "home leave," feeling isolated because we can't figure out how to articulate to friends or family that our daily life overseas–although a beautiful tapestry of vibrant markets and breathtaking moments–is also more often than not, woven with poverty, broken systems, corruption, non-potable water, family heartache, and medical scares like Malaria–realities that are far from the glamor depicted in the Netflix show, *The Diplomat.*

And yet—these experiences and years abroad have also shaped me into a woman who sees the world through a wider lens, with more discernment, confidence, and gratitude. I know how to create my own sense of stability amidst instability, and I've grown into a deeply intentional leader. I've learned how resilience is built—not by comfort, but by constant adaptation to challenging situations, navigated with courage, clarity, and conviction.

You are not waiting to become a leader—you already are one. And remember: your leadership is not just needed—it is powerful, transformative, and long overdue.

To connect with Tracy, book her for a workshop, signature talk, or to schedule a podcast interview, you can find her here on LinkedIn: linkedin.com/in/tracykmacdonald

To learn more about her travels and journey as an expatriate, follow her personal blog: carpediemcreative.com

Her writing has been published in *Bella Grace Magazine* and on Stampington & Company's blog, *Grace Notes.*

ABOUT THE AUTHOR

Tracy Macdonald hails from Columbus, Georgia, and holds a Bachelor of Arts degree in Sociology from Wesleyan College. Tracy has lived many lives—as a federal agent, consultant, diplomat, expat, public speaker, author, and mother.

Professionally, she draws on her background as a banker specializing in fraud investigations, a former Special Agent in the U.S. Secret Service, counterterrorism instructor for the Defense Intelligence Agency, and a lead consultant for Booz Allen Hamilton.

Tracy excels in dynamic situations that require innovative thinking, adaptability, resourcefulness, and strategic insight. For over a dozen years as a diplomatic spouse in the foreign service, she supported U.S. embassy missions in Eswatini, Egypt, Honduras, and Gabon. It was in these challenging environments that Tracy learned the art of reinvention and how to build stability amidst instability.

Whether she's on the TEDx stage, a podcast guest, or delivering workshops and keynotes, Tracy inspires audiences with her global journey of resilience and determination. Through story, strategy, and soulful living, she empowers others to redefine courage, transform fear, and embrace their worthiness.

Chapter 6
Corporate Entrepreneur
—Janice Marquardt

Two months before my fortieth birthday, the walls of my career as a Vice President of Supply Chain closed in. Between missing shipments from China, unpaid suppliers, and a total breakdown in communication, I was accountable for our company's supply chain failures. On a Friday afternoon, I asked my boss, the Chief Operating Officer (COO): "Do you want my resignation?"

"I'm a man of second chances," he replied. "I'll think about it."

I spent that weekend paralyzed. I was an overachiever, Type A, yet I found myself lying in bed, staring at a wall. My husband, troubled by a version of me he'd never seen in twenty-five years, called my brother. My brother told me, "Meet basic needs. Drink water. Eat. Move your body."

I followed his advice, stitched a few lines into a long-neglected quilt, and decided to face Monday without resigning. But by 10:00 AM, a chat message from my boss made the decision for me. He had flown in to "accept my verbal resignation." Within a few moments of that meeting, I was no longer employed. On paper, it was a mutual parting; in reality, I was adrift. For the first time since I was five years old, I had no "next thing." I felt broken, repeating the mantra that my career did not determine my worth, even though I didn't yet believe it. That night, I cried at group yoga class and focused on just breathing.

Two years after that day, as I sit down to write this chapter, imposter syndrome sets in. I feel unqualified. I haven't been on my own long enough. I don't have a fine-tuned marketing engine or a fleet of employees; nothing that traditionally denotes a "successful" female-owned business.

And that's just the thing.

I will never feel big enough, experienced enough, or expert enough to write this chapter. That's why I'm writing it. I may not have all the answers, but I have learned lessons worth knowing. I'm writing it precisely because I'm not so far removed from that day that I've forgotten what it's like to leave corporate life unexpectedly and without a plan. I want to share those lessons with you.

When I left corporate America after that fateful day, I didn't know what was next. My first instinct was to find my next corporate job, so I did what my career coach taught me and started networking. I set a goal of doing one networking task every weekday–five things a week. I started with what was easy. I went to tea with a staffing agency. I responded to a lunch invite from a mentee. I called my mentor from a previous company. I joined a webinar in my field and engaged in the comments section. The next week I had a first-time phone call with a long-admired network contact. I went to lunch with the Vice President of Human Resources, who left my company a few weeks before I did. I took walks. I made a wall quilt. Over the next few weeks, I applied to a few jobs and answered a few screening phone calls. I continued reaching out to people in my network, always getting a little further away from the "comfortable" contacts. And the most amazing thing happened. Each of these wonderful people asked me: Who do you need to meet? How can I support you? When will you start consulting?

This last one made me pause. Consulting? I was the breadwinner for my family and had been for sixteen years. I was Mrs. Corporate. I was good at following rules, meeting the syllabus, and checking the boxes. I was a creative thinker, but I *understood* corporate life deeply. I knew that doing favors and making allies who would say my name when the executives were talking about who to promote was how to play politics. I knew that putting in an IT ticket if I needed a new headset was how to navigate bureaucracy. I knew to keep a neutral gray blazer hanging on the coat hook of my cubicle so I could walk into an executive meeting at any time and "look professional." One of my best friends' sons had even described the university I went to as "too corporate" on a college visit. I never considered being an entrepreneur. That word was terrifying.

However, that word "entrepreneur" kept coming up. So I did what I usually do when faced with something new: I looked for a way to learn how to do it. I explored a couple of programs and joined one called Consulting Success, which was a mix of one-on-one coaching and group calls, along with a library of how-to videos and an online messenger board community. I started figuring out the answers to the most important questions:

Who am I?

Who do I help?

With what problem?

The answers to these have changed over time, but my current version is something like: *I help operations leaders elevate their supply chains to build value.* Sometimes it's: *I bring negotiation back into procurement.* If I'm at a casual cocktail party, it's simply: *I solve supply chain problems.* A professional friend of mine in Human Resources says: *I help founders and CEOs build high-performing teams and fix leadership gaps.* Another professional contact who coaches executives tells people: *I help people lead better and live better.* Someone who helped women organize might say: *I help mothers tame the chaos of #momlife.* The point is always for the person I'm talking to say, "Oh! That's me! I have supply chain problems!" or "I want to fix my leadership gaps!" or "I don't know, there's a LOT of chaos in my life to tame!"

I started telling everyone in my network who I was, who I helped, and with what problem. I started writing my book, <u>Transform Procurement: The Value of E-auctions</u>. I wrote articles on LinkedIn and published them, faithfully, every week. I felt like I was shouting into the void. But then I started getting calls. Friends of friends. Professional contacts of people I had lunch with said, "I have a supply chain problem. Can you help?" I learned how to market the problems I solve instead of my skills and write a client proposal focused on value.

My husband helped me name my company, Passwall Solutions. We have always been very geeky people, and Passwall is the name of a magic spell in Dungeons and Dragons. The passwall spell makes a door through a wall of stone, creating a new passage. In corporate life, the supply chain can be like a wall with no door, so I help people make a door in that wall.

My first client needed help and found me through my network. They had exactly one procurement team member handling billions of dollars in purchases. He used to be part of a team of four or five, but the rest of his team quit or were let go. He didn't speak "executive" fluently and was sending nitty gritty details down to the penny to the company's COO. The COO wanted to consider hiring me, but I wasn't sure if I could rejoin the corporate world.

I didn't know what I was doing and felt like an imposter, but I kept going. I started by evaluating their supply chain, strengths and weaknesses, from demand to warehousing. I built what is now my Supply Chain 360 Assessment from scratch. I represented that client's procurement team in an important presentation to their end customer. At the end of that presentation, the COO turned to me and said, "You brought so much more than procurement to this event." That simple sentence of support meant everything to me. I could do it. My corporate experience *was* relevant. When my network brought me my next phone call, I was ready to answer with the confidence I built through my first client. I could help.

Now that I'm a few years into this journey, I have seven key lessons to share that have helped me succeed as an entrepreneur. May these lessons be of value to someone starting on a path like mine:

1. **Your "ideal client" may not be who you think it is.** At first, I thought I would help supply chain leaders. It turns out, the person who hires me is actually *their boss*. While I

help the supply chain leader solve problems, they don't typically ask for help, don't recognize they need help, or are too prideful to admit someone from the outside *can* help. I understand that. I was there myself. If you're just starting out as a consultant after being someone who had a role in the field, recognize you may have to change your target audience. I have yet to have a client hire me who was the supply chain manager at their organization. If I were in healthcare, it wouldn't be the doctor who hired me; it would be the hospital director. If I were helping clients with addiction recovery, the person calling me might be their psychologist or even their attorney. The person I help is not necessarily the one who writes the check.

2. **Know that you *can* do it.** Borrow the faith of others if you're having trouble believing in yourself for a little while. Surround yourself with people who believe in you. Join groups of people who have been there and will share their wisdom; I promise they are out there (shout out to my sisters from the North American Women Business Owners/NAWBO!). My tipping point was when my stepfather told me he couldn't think of someone better positioned to start their own business than me. He was one of many, but his vote of confidence was the one that triggered me to start building. While a close family member may not seem like part of a professional network, they surely can be!

3. **Network, network, network.** Register for that small business lunch-and-learn, no matter what topic they are discussing. Come early and linger past the end if your schedule allows. Walk up to people and be honest about how you're feeling. You will be shocked at how your vulnerability is rewarded. Introduce yourself and follow up with, "I'm not really sure what I'm doing here, but I'm interested in learning." Work out a few answers to the question "What do you do?" that focus on the problem you

solve. Adjust your answer if it doesn't resonate with people. Ask people what they do and what problems they are facing. Be interested in the answer. If socializing like this is especially draining for you, schedule some time at home with a book that afternoon or whatever your desired wind-down activity is. Put time on your calendar to pause and celebrate your bravery because that level of vulnerability can be *hard*. I feel like I accidentally stumbled into networking as the first step to building my business, and that first week of networking led me to my first few clients.

4. **Learn to say Yes.** Try things that are a bit new. Once you've built a framework, model, training program, etc., for one client/customer, you can use it for others. If you think something is within your ability to accomplish, it probably is. You might find you like that task. You might also find that you're only ever going to do it once. When a company reached out to me and wanted me to record video training for them in my area of expertise, I said yes. That whole adventure led me to Dubai to record training sessions during the largest flood in Dubai's history. It was an adventure and a mind-blowing experience, and it happened because I said yes. Of course, saying "yes" too much can lead to the dreaded burnout, which is why my next lesson was learning to say no.

5. **Learn to say No.** There's only one of you. There is more to life than being a founder. You may have family members who need to be cared for. You will always have yourself to care for. One of the best pieces of information I received early on is that a consultant or contractor is fully booked if they are working about twenty-six hours each week on client work. Twenty-six! My initial reaction: what am I doing with the other fourteen?! Or more realistically, the other twenty-four?! The answer, of course, is working on my business. Marketing. Networking. Building my authority by writing articles or books. Planning and goal-

setting for my next step or next big dream. I made the mistake about a year into running my business that many people make at some point: I said yes to a client when my answer should have been no. While I could do what they needed done and did get them the results they wanted, they *actually* wanted someone to sit in a chair in their office (a three-hour plane flight away from me) and run their team for forty hours a week. If it weren't for the distance, this might have worked. Ultimately, I don't really *want* to devote all of my time to one client. They basically wanted me to rejoin the corporate world, and I didn't want to do that. So I should have said no, and instead I endured six months refusing their request for me to come sit in a chair at their headquarters. I was wasting time with that client.

6. **Spend your time on the tasks that move the needle.** Whatever you spend your time doing, focus on the tasks that add value to your life or your business over the ones that burn you out and bring little value. In every business, there are ten-dollar tasks (responding to basic emails, scheduling meetings, booking travel, recording labor hours), hundred-dollar tasks (bookkeeping, posting or responding to social media, managing suppliers), and thousand-dollar tasks (developing products, presenting proposals, writing marketing materials). Figure out which tasks fall in what category for your business, and spend as much time as possible doing the thousand-dollar tasks. Outsource the hundred-dollar and ten-dollar tasks wherever you can. The first person I hired to help my business was a contractor for two-and-a-half hours per week to complete administrative work. She found the open times in the *five* calendars I was managing, entered my hours into tracking so I could figure out where my most value-added time was, and published my weekly articles. Those two-and-a-half hours per week made a huge difference in my ability to focus on tasks for clients and my business.

7. **Know how to calculate the value you bring.** One advantage of being in the supply chain is that we are trained from day one to calculate our value. Procurement or supply chain team member annual bonuses are often based on cost savings, lead time reductions, and supplier quality improvements. Sales team members are similarly trained to calculate value by earning commissions based on sales numbers and meeting targets. If you come from an industry that doesn't emphasize the monetary value of your work, figure out how to convert what you do into bottom-line dollars. If you work with people, perhaps that value is in reduced turnover or lower training costs. If you work in process improvement, your value proposition may be time and labor savings. If you work with customer service, perhaps you reduce the cost of sales or improve a brand's goodwill. Whatever you do, figure out a way to assign a dollar value to it. Then, base your pricing off that value.

The guideline I have used from that early consulting coaching is to make your fees twenty percent of the value you will bring the organization (also known as a return on investment or ROI of five-hundred percent). I confess I am still not always good at this, partly because in the supply chain it's very common to work with extremely large numbers. I implemented a program for one of my clients with a 25,000% return on investment from my fee in the first year alone. While the results for this client were even better than my best estimates, I still raised my fees for the next client (but not quite to five-hundred percent ROI).

Today, there is more support for women owning their own businesses and blazing their own paths than there has been at any other time in history. That being said, it's okay to feel like it's harder than it has to be. Sometimes I feel guilty that it's hard. After all, haven't we "solved" the fact that women historically had to be attached to a husband, father, or brother to have our own bank accounts, apply for our own loans, and simply manage our own lives? Doesn't that mean everything is fair and it's up to us to build our businesses and cover the remaining gaps? This is kind of true, but it's still hard to be taken seriously as a female entrepreneur. There is a quiet assumption that running our own businesses is something we do *in between* raising our children, putting dinner on the table, and caring for our aging parents. It's our side hustle. Our extra spending money. This attitude persists even when we out-earn our spouses, whether as an entrepreneur or in the corporate world. While we are no longer told we cannot be in the room because we are women, the personal networks of the people in power are still mostly straight, white, middle-aged men. When a CEO looks to his network to find his next board member, he's more likely to call someone who looks like him. This is why it's so important that *we* become CEOs, founders, and entrepreneurs.

I have out-earned my husband for every year of our marriage, and it has never bothered him. He is my best cheerleader, advocate, and support on every level. Even so, my family tends to forget that I *work* when I work from home. I had to lease an office space to be able to de-center my family life and get work done. After the first week and a half of going into my office, my family discovered we had no clean towels because I was not quietly moving laundry all day. I note all of this as a reminder that it's normal to struggle differently as women on our own, even when surrounded by a loving, supportive network. Be where you are, do what you need to do, and give yourself some grace for the fact that it's hard.

I wish you the absolute best, whether you are a founder, support a founder, or simply enjoy watching founders. Know deeply who you help and who hires you, and especially know that you can do it. Network your way into wild opportunities that make you eager to say yes, but don't be afraid to say no. Spend your own time wisely and on the tasks that truly build value for you and your customers, and know that I am cheering you on every step of the way.

Photo credit: Sourcing Industry Group (SIG)

ABOUT THE AUTHOR

Like many supply chain professionals, **Janice Marquardt** never planned to be in procurement. She was an engineer, and that second major in communication studies was there just for balance. When she needed a graceful way out of a political career situation, she found herself in a role as an Engineering Buyer and also found her calling. From there, Janice became a commodity manager and then moved to a senior buyer role at a large utility company. Over nine years, she moved into Procurement Manager, Director of Global Procurement, and then Vice President of Supply Chain roles, including building teams and processes using her engineering problem-solving skills. She lives on a farm west of Des Moines, Iowa, with her husband, two children, one Great Pyrenees dog, five cats, two dozen Belted Galloway "Oreo" cows, and about forty chickens.

Janice founded Passwall Solutions in 2023. The company focuses on solving supply chain problems and helping supply chain teams create and capture value. Passwall Solutions has helped multiple clients elevate their procurement teams from simply cutting POs to truly strategic sourcing and has guided multi-billion-dollar e-auction program implementations. Janice regularly publishes articles to her website on a variety of topics in supply chain, entrepreneurship, and leadership.

Janice can be reached on LinkedIn, at Janice@passwallsolutions.com or her website, www.passwallsolutions.com.

Chapter 7
I Beg You To Differ
—Diana Frank

To my 15-year-young self:

Believe it or not, it will all make sense. The hard things. The sadness. The inner bewilderment with this world around you. Friendships that will last far beyond family. You will meet Ute, Lotte, and Urs. And like the fairy in Cinderella, they have three gifts for you. Embrace them. And there will be nothing you cannot be.

For everyone else:

The most impactful moments in my professional life were never the things I accomplished. It was the privilege to witness when seemingly small things meant the world to someone. When they felt seen for who they are and what they are capable of. When "I can't" turned into "I can see this is possible." And the biggest gifts I got? When people saw me as a person. Recognized strengths and talents I might not have seen that way.

MOST PEOPLE DON'T GET ME...

As someone who sees structures and patterns, who thinks in systems and who senses the energy in the room, I learned early on: just because it's obvious to me doesn't mean people understand it or can relate to my way of seeing the world.

Most people learn from examples and role models. I observed my environment, and it made no sense to me. So I tried to explain the world to myself. I questioned a lot and figured whatever it is, I cannot follow if it doesn't feel right for me.

I read biographies. Gandhi impressed me greatly, not for his sacrifices or achievements, but for his clarity: he liked many things in other religions, and if Christianity were just the Sermon on the Mount, he would convert right away. Yet there was also the history of the church. I agreed: there is no such thing as the one right thing. There is always context, culture, and circumstances. There are values and valuable things to learn. And I am the one who defines what matters to me. So I started to cherry-pick my own value system from everything I could lay my hands on.

I was about 13 when I stopped telling people what I was interested in. It was way too weird being questioned in the school library because of the books I wanted to read. I went to the public library instead, and to adult education courses for psychology and philosophy. Kudos to my mom. She did not get me at all; she opted out of school as soon as she could, yet she respected my wish to do this. In hindsight, I suspect she found it easier to give in than to try to reason with me.

I DON'T FIT INTO BOXES

Many people need boxes, the familiar, to sort people into structures they understand so they can relate to them. I don't need that kind of sorting system to sort things out.

There is one box I can relate to, though: the oldest daughter. The substitute parent for her siblings. Taking on responsibilities way too early. Often not because she is forced to, but because she can and it feels like the right thing to do. That was me.

Do women see this as leading already? Many don't. While it's a testament to self-leadership, those who are used to taking on responsibilities are leading. You step up. You decide.. You choose what you stand for. If you make yourself do it, no one can make you. You own it. There is pride in being capable.

Yet there is a trap: taking on what is not yours to carry, just because you can.

Uncomfortable truth: you lead, or you follow. You're in control, or you're not. And you get to choose who has power over you.

The last part is hard. People only have power over you if you give it to them. Are you too young to learn this at 14? Absolutely. And I cannot say how proud I am of my younger self when she refused to become a victim, no matter what. This laid the foundation for my inner authority and integrity. Regardless of being scared, I knew: this is the only way to live, on my terms.

THE CURSE AND BLESSING OF THE CAPABLE WOMAN

Fast forward 8 years. Now 23 years young.

My first job outside family business and tutoring. A flyer at my university: multimedia production company looking for talented students. I had no idea what "multimedia" even meant in 1994. I started as the 8th member. No structures in place. A super ambitious business owner who enjoyed having a sparring partner for his ideas, who did not care about long days.

When it came to figuring things out on the go, I never had a hard time. What I learned: not everyone can handle uncertainty easily. That directly led to my first informal leadership role.

We got a small project. And a deadline. A colleague and I. She was older, working full-time. Yet it was obvious this was over her head. So I created my first project plan ever, feeling bad that I should be telling her what to do. Instead of anger, I got a hug and a super-relieved colleague saying, "Finally, someone here tells me what to do." I was shocked.

Interestingly, when precision mattered, those things often landed on my desk. This is how I ended up doing the pilot project for one of the very first online banking solutions for Deutsche Bank. One-week deadline. I was away at a conference for half the time. The designer had a meltdown. My boss was stressed and busy. When I came back, I had 3.5 days left. My boss saw what I prepared 15 minutes before the meeting.

We presented in the office of a Deutsche Bank VP. I answered questions. Handled follow-ups.

In the taxi back, my boss went silent. That angry silence. Then: "What are you thinking, telling a client something 'can't be done'?"

I was so tired I couldn't make sense of it. So I called the assistant to the VP.

"If I behaved inappropriately, I just got severely reprimanded, and I'd really like to apologize."

He had no idea what I was talking about. Then he said something I've never forgotten: "You told us your honest opinion. That's what we pay you for. Everything else we can do ourselves."

That day I learned: it's not serving a client to just do what they ask for. And the good ones know the difference.

In the end, we won the project. The first 1M Deutsche Mark contract for the company.

A PATTERN ON REPEAT

Fast forward another few years. I had a reputation: if things got difficult, she would manage. What actually happened: I fixed not-well-thought-through concepts.

During a freelance job, a colleague told me I would do a better job thinking about requirements and customer needs than the people hired for it. I agreed, yet I did not feel like I would formally qualify, and I was never asked to do it.

Now, when I am writing this, this is such a female thing to do, waiting to be asked and to be invited.

He introduced me to project work in IT. I happened to be the only female on the entire floor. My team lead told me he really wanted a woman on the team, so this was how I got my first job as a user experience expert.

When it came to renewing the contract, three other teams wanted the same. My pride in all my wonderful skills, out of the window, replaced by: as long as she is a woman.

What actually happened: this was about a missing energy.

TOTALLY UNRELATED?

Somewhere in between projects, a new neighbor moved in. Ute. One day, she mentioned, "You can tell me everything, because you never judge. And you leave it to me what I do with it."

What a strange thing to say. There is no other way, right?!

It took me about 15 years to fully understand the gift Ute gave me that day: a deep understanding of this is special.

Not long after, Lotte, my auntie, 50 years older: "With you, I just can be who I am. I don't need to worry what you think. That means a lot to me."

I felt honored. Yet I did not really get the deeper meaning until many years later: She felt seen for who she really is.

YEARS PASSED, AND I WENT NOWHERE

Roles became more demanding, projects more complex. I often got assignments when it was not about the best skill match, but rather when they could not find anyone who had done it before.

When initial trust was needed, "she will figure it out," those projects came to me. Yet always only on a tactical and operational level.

What I did not see for a long time: I was way too valuable fixing things and delivering solutions.

I was asked to do the uncomfortable because I could cope with it. Today, I see the power dynamics behind that. Why change the way you work if you get away with it? Val, our lead developer, once mentioned: "They have no idea how much money you save them because you address future problems before they surface."

I love leverage. And I don't like to feel like I let people down. This combination, working hard on things that don't make sense and still feeling responsible, slowly drained me. What starts as "it's not too bad, and hey, I can deal with it" might be the most dangerous state. Not because it's bad. Because it's not bad enough to do something about it.

What happened instead: I got tired and grumpy.

I learned just how grumpy one evening, when I met Urs, who traveled to Zürich just to have dinner with me. All I did was rant and complain. He gave me the space, endured me. When we walked back to my hotel, I finally realized: I am not the kind of person who complains. And here I was.

I apologized. He hugged me. "It's ok."

Little did I know this was the last time I would see him. His cancer came back fast.

One part of me still grieves how I used that evening with a wonderful soul. The larger part is endlessly grateful for Urs's gift: showing me how we sacrifice ourselves in the name of service, while doing ourselves, and the people we claim to love, the greatest disservice.

GIVING MYSELF A BREAK

Shortly after this dinner, long before I knew what would happen to Urs, I decided, whatever I do, if it turns me into such an angry person that I do not even recognize myself anymore, it's time to stop.

I knew all the things I would not do anymore: Not firefighting in projects, not an agency model, not a consultancy model, not company politics, no hidden agendas.

Instead of what I **can** do, figuring out what I actually **want** to do.

Where is the leverage?

What fuels me and brings me joy?

Sometimes I think I unlearned how to want, to wish, to dream when I was super young. You make yourself useful to be tolerated at the table. It's an extremely uncomfortable truth to see how long I lived by this idea.

I was always my own person, never backed down from what I knew to be true. **AND** I did not ask for what I needed.

So I gave myself a budget and an intention: to explore, further and beyond.

And one strict rule: No business, no important decisions, not taking on another project, no matter what. For one year.

GOING FULL CIRCLE

I joined two high-ticket programs, one training and one about business development, and I was shocked. While I joined out of curiosity, others quit their jobs for the marketing promise. I observed that no one worked directly with the people; everyone went through classroom modules on their own. I saw people becoming increasingly devastated, blaming themselves because they could not make it work for them.

If this were what it would take to have a 'scalable business,' I wouldn't have one.

I started mentoring some, helping them put things into perspective: "This is not on you, this is what you thought would be part of it, and it's not there: the care, the working on your business and how to make it work."

In parallel, I went through two coaching certification programs.

And something super strange happened. Ute's and Lotte's words came back to me. And it's been the exact thing I've been hearing over and over.

The coaching part: It felt like home. Asking questions? And asking questions differently? I can do that. Yet more importantly, I will know if what you answer is true to you, even if you don't allow yourself to see it this way yet. And once you know what you want, we will find ways. My inner pathfinder, my strategist, my love to see you thrive, all here for you. Because this is it: nothing fuels me more than seeing people who dare to own who they are and conquer the world on their terms.

Some months into my sabbatical, I stumbled over a personal strengths assessment.

The results: no surprise at all.

Primary:

Strategist, Philomath, Coach, Storyteller, Commander

Secondary:

Problem Solver, Thinker, Empathizer, Deliverer, Catalyst

Yet seeing those strengths put into two different categories, there was no way to unsee them. She solves problems and delivers. Super useful in projects. Why waste those talents when she is perfect to execute? That hit hard.

In that minute, I knew: my secondary strengths must be off the table. They're too tempting and would take me straight back to where I've been before. They also undermine what I need most when working with people: Eye level and their maturity to be responsible for their own results.

I FINALLY GET WHY THEY DON'T GET ME...

It took me writing this chapter to see why I seem to confuse so many people.

Growing up in a family with no men present for almost two generations, I do not think in classic gender categories. My grandmother had a clear understanding that some tasks are for men only. When my grandfather died young, there was no man left. So it was either my auntie or me who was assigned to those tasks. I figured it out. I always saw it as a privilege that no one ever told me, "You cannot do this," or "this is not for girls."

While I always saw myself as a woman, I also never understood why being a woman is supposed to have any influence on what I do and how.

I never thought about leadership in categories. I just led the way that made sense to me. Only in the last few years have I started to look at male and female energies. I realized: I've always used both equally. Which thoroughly confused my environment, not because it didn't make sense, but because it didn't meet expectations.

I always had a natural blindness to assumed power dynamics. Not as rebellion. Just nothing that registered in my system. For me, authority comes from clarity and lived experience. Not from titles. I would question decisions without acknowledging rank, and I would hold complexity when others wanted simplicity.

But organizations don't want complexity. They want simplified structures. And I kept not understanding that it wasn't about building sensible organizations with people who are doing well. It was more often about preserving power structures.

I looked into the leadership qualities I have and how they are commonly labeled:

- Strategic/systems thinking (often coded masculine)
- Deep alignment sensing (often coded feminine)
- Direct truth-telling (masculine)
- Holding space/keeping people safe enough (feminine)
- Rational frameworks/processes (masculine)
- Intuitive pattern recognition (feminine)

This makes exactly half of the qualities coded as "male" and half as "female." Yes, I have high standards AND care deeply. Serve clarity and precision with humor. And hold my boundaries without retreat.

No wonder people are confused. They expect: tough OR caring. Not both.

IT'S OKAY NOT TO MEET EXPECTATIONS

Guess I always knew that. And I never tried to. At least not others' expectations. My own, that's an entirely different story.

My truth: Why would I pretend to be someone to get something that I actually don't want?

And my genuine bewilderment: Why would anyone choose that over what actually works, or at least has the potential to work?

Benefit of being an external expert: You see the patterns on repeat. You see what would work, yet is not wanted. You observe the power plays. There are leaders who never hear the truth because either people want to look good in front of them, or fear that the messenger gets killed.

And there is a reason why so many try to step out of those structures lately.

For many, starting something on their own feels like the next step to take. I met some of these people in programs I signed up for. And learned: most of them tried to create a new job for themselves, not a business. They did not look into what they personally want or what really drives them, but rather at what someone would pay for.

None of the programs I joined out of curiosity cared for people in a way that felt sensible or responsible. They mostly focused on operational skills; no one looked into actual business development for the people.

BUILDING CIRCLES

Nobody was asking first: "Who are YOU in your business?"

This question became the beginning of my first community. Looking at personal strengths, people's wants and needs, and their circumstances to build the foundations of their business.

It turned out to be a core question most people never answered.

What started as a place to bring together people I met along my own journey, while quietly stopping to "help" behind the scenes, became a second home. A place where people felt someone was truly listening, and where like-minded souls came together who prefer to build and grow their business on their own terms. A place where I did not need to explain myself and could be of service while gaining visibility and showing authority in a deeply human, connected way.

This community grew to over 250 people in the first year, building connections and laying the foundation for lifelong friendships. The kind of "you know when you know" friendships are built on mutual support and the willingness to nudge each other to do even better. The best thing about building alongside others: you learn from observation and felt experience, and you benefit from each other's strengths. When you build in public, you directly see what works and what does not.

One of my coachees mentioned that she was surprised by how transparent I am about the steps I take, even the ones that did not work as expected. The core of this feedback was her deep sense of relief: yes, it is okay if I have not figured it out yet. Getting better while you follow your path is the best you can do. Period. There is always time to adjust. And I am not the only one.

OWNING A BUSINESS IS OFTEN LONELY

Not being seen for who you are while you are building is one of the hardest things to cope with.

I often have been this confidant, the person people can trust. I never thought it would become the one asset that makes the difference. When they feel seen for who they are, with someone on their side to go through risks and fears before they surface.

If you've been told you're complicated, what could be true instead:

The structures you're being measured against have been too small.

This is my invitation: Find your circles.

If it feels like they are missing: build them!

I BEG YOU TO DIFFER

Make a difference. Not to be different, but to respect what you really want and need.

Stop waiting to be invited to tables where people don't make space for you. Stop proving yourself in ways that no longer matter. Start being yourself.

There is always only ONE way: the path we walk.

Who am I?

What matters most to me?

What do I want to be remembered for?

Your people are there, waiting for you to dare to step out and show up, so they have a chance to find you.

That's your obligation, to people who need someone to go first, to show another way to build without shrinking your seeing, or apologizing for your clarity.

The tax I pay willingly: Setting tables rather than waiting for invitations. Being visible. Building circles where authority comes from clarity.

Every person who:

- Stops rescuing missions they weren't allowed to shape
- Stops being tactically useful while remaining strategically invisible
- Stops stretching themselves thin for advice that wasn't built for their circumstances
- Steps up to be what they're actually here for

This is what becomes possible when we stop waiting to be invited and start building our own circles.

~

Connect with Diana
www.linkedin.com/in/frankdiana
www.instagram.com/dianafrank.official/
www.youtube.com/@DianaFrank-UA
www.skool.com/advantage

ABOUT THE AUTHOR

Diana Frank is a strategist, trusted advisor, and author. She works with executives, company owners, and generational leaders on the brink of decisions where authorship and clarity define what comes next. Her driving question is simple: **Who are YOU in your business?**

She explores with you **YOUR** way forward, based on what you want and what matters most to you.

More than two decades in product and service development, customer experience, and strategic transformation across automotive (BMW Partner, MAN), insurance (Allianz, Munich Re), finance (Deutsche Bank, Raiffeisen Bank), logistics (Deutsche Bahn), and global events (FIFA World Cup, UEFA Euro, Olympic Games) shaped Diana's ability to hold complexity while valuing human-centered solutions over systems.

As founder of **UNFAIR ADVANTAGE**, she focuses on what others often overlook: the ability to listen to your inner compass and the power in what makes you different. Known for bringing "clarity with humor," she works with clients 1:1 and in her communities, where people are seen for who they are.

Chapter 8
Grit-to-Grace

—Dr. Katherine Humphreys

As the oldest child and only girl in a middle-class family, my mother instilled in me a three-tiered survival strategy: Plan A, Plan B, and a back-up Plan C. For an "achiever" personality type, planning wasn't just about to become my habit; it would be my shield, giving me the confidence to continually push forward. My family line had exposure to education, but not a 4-year degree so earning mine became my first major life objective.

STRATEGY 1: SETTING THE FOUNDATION

I helped pay for school as a partially-funded athlete and went on to a master's degree by working in athletics, then entered the career field with the aim of an Athletic Director Position (coincidentally a very male-oriented field).

As I was learning the politics of Athletics, an opportunity emerged to pivot into University Admissions and Enrollment; this new field was complex and interesting, involved helping others obtain the goal of a college-degree, and had a business aspect that I really enjoyed. But soon, "The Plan" hit a wall.

At a top-tier research university, I found myself sitting across from a new boss who was a fish out of water. He wasn't asking questions to learn our culture; he was asking them to learn the job itself. As I sat there explaining the basic mechanics of our department, it became crystal clear: I was training my superior. In the coming weeks, he would ask me what to do in the face of each decision he should make. I would sit in meetings hearing my words coming out of his mouth. He was the puppet; I was the puppet-master, the Oz behind the curtain of his facade. I had hit the glass ceiling. Twice, I applied for the corner office I had already been running in an interim capacity. Twice, a male candidate who "fit the mold" ultimately received the nod.

STRATEGY 2: ACCEPTANCE AND REPOSITIONING

When faced with a plateau you can either be defeated or accept the reality. I was staring down the barrel of at least another few years of running the show as the Associate Director, without the Senior title or pay. I confess I felt hurt and frustrated. However, I didn't plan to sit long with those feelings. I like to quickly strategize what is needed in order to make sure my life outcomes are not set on repeat. I planned to STEP UP to do even more.

The Flex:

- I chose to develop and implement new initiatives around the quality of our services. This involved spending months shadowing every unit to collect data points, then incorporating those into metrics the teams could continue to gather on their own.
- I wrote myself into lunch-time and Friday coverage schedules in order to regularly sit in the "hot seats," and face the challenges of any front-line staff.
- I developed feedback surveys and interviewed students. Then met regularly to review with all of the feeder units that had direct hand-offs to/from our functions. This helped

us all to learn what our "customers" wanted and needed at a granular level.

The Outcome:

- One of the advantages to women in leadership roles is that we bring compassion. Compassion comes from understanding; knowing what it is like to be operating ALL aspects of the business, walking in the shoes of all those we will be interacting with and leading. Compassion can also be a strategic advantage. When you walk in the shoes of every person you lead, your authority becomes indisputable. I made sure that everything I was doing would have benefits in general, all the while contributing to my own ongoing development.

STRATEGY 3: STRENGTHENING CREDENTIALS

Anyone faced with determining if further education will get them to the place they want should consider all options for reaching the goal. Sometimes, more life experience, time in the chosen field, and getting to know the right people will push open the door without the cost of an educational investment. Maybe just a strategic class or two or a certification will do the trick. For me, obtaining the highest degree in a career field that was focused on academics combined with years of experience in that field could equal a profile that no hiring committee could overlook.

The Flex:

- If the glass ceiling is reinforced, credentials become your sledgehammer. I decided to pursue a PhD; not just for the title, but to walk the same intense path as the faculty I led. This was a massive investment of time and money, balanced against a new marriage and a biological clock that was poised to start ticking.

The Outcome:

- You don't always climb the mountain because you want to; you climb it because you need the view from the top to be taken seriously by those standing on the peak.

STRATEGY 4: INDISPENSABILITY

Define your value so clearly that it becomes your unmistakable professional signature. This doesn't always require being overt or loud; it means becoming the person whose presence is essential for the best and most informed decisions to be made. We achieve this by thinking beyond our own tasks to understand the systemic web of their impact. We don't just envision the big picture; we map out the terrain and execute the necessary steps to bring that vision to life.

The Flex:

- Identify an area where other leaders are lacking. In my field, this was an in-depth knowledge of the technical systems behind the work being done. Indispensability looked like volunteering to head a massive state-wide system integration while others stayed in their silos. I didn't just want to see the new software; I wanted to understand how a single data point in Admissions traveled all the way to a student's graduation day and beyond.

The Outcome:

- This Project Lead role not only put me in a position of importance and decision-making, it also put me in the room "where it happens," so to speak. I was meeting frequently with those at the president's cabinet level and leadership across multiple institutions. It felt comfortable, like this is where I belong. I was traveling with senior leadership to other states that had implemented similar systems. This meant I was at dinners and on planes where true relationship building occurred. I became *indispensable* on the project and it was a natural progression for that momentum to propel me to the next level and into the senior leadership role.

STRATEGY 5: STRATEGIC PARTNERING

A benefit of a long climb up the ladder is the *opportunity* to build community, support, and alliances. Even if you're not working within the structure of a broad organization, there is the potential to network in your field. In my organization the hiring of higher leadership involved multiple committees, multi-day interviews, presentations, and gathering of feedback and input from a large consortium. If you're working independently or starting a business, there is still some community you need buy-in from. Beyond academia, this may look like nurturing ties with stakeholders, vendors and future customers.

The Flex:

- Go to more events, join more committees, say 'yes' to even more opportunities. I was insanely busy, but recognized this as a moment in time. I had a mission. I took the helm of the Commencement Committee which had such broad exposure it stretched my leadership skills to far-reaching corners of the campus and the local community. I went to every faculty-senate meeting and spoke up and contributed.

The Outcome:

- I was building a network and gathering my supporters so that the next time my name was up for the role, there'd be more people who could confidently say, "Yes, she knows what she is doing; she deserves our vote."

STRATEGY 6: NURTURE THE BACK-UP PLANS

We can be caught in the juxtaposition between whole-heartedly believing we'll get what we want and pursuing as such, and the fact life does not always go exactly as planned (and sometimes that can be a good thing). Whether you are positioning yourself for an opening in your company, preparing to take the leap to something new, or preparing to start a business, it can be a good idea to explore all the angles and maybe even keep several parallel paths open.

The Flex:

- When an opportunity came to bridge a gap in my field, I took it and I started a training business with some of my doctoral contacts. We wrote a book, secured contracts across the nation, and were plenary speakers at major conferences.
- When years of presenting and holding leadership roles within a national organization led to consulting offers, I took them.
- With a passion for real estate, I explored ways to invest in owning multiple homes and became certified as a property manager.

The Outcome:

- I complimented my journey to give myself other avenues and options to pursue as well.

STRATEGY 7: SEIZING THE DAY

These back-up plans weren't intended to usurp my intention of getting to the helm. I completed my doctorate on an accelerated timeline while marrying and welcoming two children. This was an intense period. My Mom paused her life in another state and moved in with us initially to provide support with my first infant. Later, my already-busy husband would step up even more, cooking dinner while I was stuck in traffic. There were some really raw moments where I sat at the kitchen counter trying to learn advanced statistics, sobbing from a combination of exhaustion and not understanding the topic matter. One of my children had been born the morning after I gutted my way through comprehensive exams. The second came the morning after I defended my dissertation. Later, I walked across the graduation stage to be hooded and then immediately had to leave the ceremony to feed my infant. I was impressed that I survived.

I now had higher credentials, more knowledge, and a broader network. It was time to face the hardest hurdle for me personally: PRIDE. I stood at a crossroads: back down to protect my ego, or hold my head up high and risk a third public rejection. The voices in my head were loud. They whispered that I was "Pathetic for trying for the same role again ("would I ever learn?")." They asked if "I had no shame in pursuing a door that had been slammed in my face twice before?" I reflected on the stinging silence of the previous two "no's" and the way it felt to walk back into the office the next day and continue working for the men who got "my" job.

The Flex:

- There is something about being so sure that you can do well in a job that will shine through. Your brilliance won't necessarily be recognized right away. Continue to be brilliant anyway.
- This was about endurance. I chose to believe that my worth wasn't defined by the University's past decisions but my current readiness. I prepared for the third interview, not with the desperation of someone who needed the job but the quiet confidence of someone who had done it. I walked into the campus presentations not as an applicant hoping for a chance, but as the only sensible solution.

The Outcome:

- A beautiful thing about obtaining a promotion after two previous tries is that YOU know you earned it. You really know the job well, you showed you have fight when others may have fled. By staying, I demonstrated grit and was humble in the face of almighty rejection. I had won additional allies and believers along the way. Now was the time to put my strategies to the test.
- I set about rewriting some of the unspoken, male-enforced rules. I worked hard to be open to the needs of the families of both the men and women in our office.
- I loved serving as the senior leader and I tried to use the privilege to promote others based on both merit as well as intangible strengths like emotional intelligence and character.
- I looked for growth opportunities for everyone (many of the same opportunities that I had sought for myself) and encouraged team members to pursue paths they were passionate about.
- I practiced a collaborative leadership style, moving away from a command-and-control mode to one of shared ownership. I sought to bring everyone to the table and utilized modalities that encouraged debate and consensus.
- I put an emphasis on team-building and smooth collaboration with other areas.
- I instituted an internal committee charged with making "fun" a normal part of our work-life and culture through regular board game days and office olympics, dress-up days, and celebrations.

STEP 8: GRACE

I would be remiss in implying the struggles were over. In my tenure I faced challenges related to being judged for my femininity, wardrobe, and even the car I drove. I experienced sexual harassment. There were internal HR issues. I had to dig deeper than I felt equipped to try to help and support employees who were dealing with mental health and other issues. I had to fight to be taken seriously in rooms that were often filled with more men than women. I would discreetly handle leaking breasts during meetings and the mental anguish of having others in charge of the care of my young children. I did not always get it right, I was constantly learning and I was challenged daily. Yet, I am certain of this: *Women deserve the same opportunity to lead our workplaces and inspire our future generations.*

The Flex:

- Part of leadership is knowing when to step aside. My transition to the senior role was fairly seamless because I had spent years already doing the work, but the corner office was never my finish line. Because the climb was such a hard-won fight, I felt I had earned the right to dictate my next move. I had exercised every ounce of grit I possessed, and in doing so, I discovered my agency: the absolute freedom to choose my own path. I had the degrees and the miles behind me to do whatever I wanted next.

- After a few years serving at the helm, I visited HR. I learned my position level and years of service meant I could retire early with benefits. I could also apply for and demonstrate that I was deserving of Faculty Emeritus status (which I now proudly hold). I held long discussions with my husband and financial advisor and determined it made sense to let go.

The Outcome:

- This wasn't particularly easy. It was uncomfortable and sometimes still is but I have total flexibility now, and my children hardly remember "Corporate Mom." My subsequent chapters have involved consulting, entrepreneurialism, traveling to over forty-five countries, living abroad, writing, and helping others share their stories. My future plans are to increase my volunteerism and find ways to serve my community, learn new skills and try things I have never tried before. I have a long list of experiences from which to draw. I have always had a Plan A, B, and C and now is the time for Plan Me.

FINAL MESSAGE

I had pushed myself hard, maybe too hard, and exhaustion or burnout were probably just around the corner (it's a good thing to recognize that and try to get ahead of it). Looking back, even just taking one or two of these steps may have been adequate. None of us needs to sacrifice all of ourselves for work. Consider my path one of suggestions; ideas or inspiration for an approach to getting to where you would like to go.

I am a female who led and persisted. We can all do something for the women and daughters that come after us. We can *each* play a part in breaking through the glass, paving the path, and handing over something that is theirs to define. Don't back down from a leadership position or business opportunity that you want. Don't let a "no" be the outcome you sit with. Instead, let others benefit from your perspective at the leadership table. Let others see what it looks like to really want something and go for it despite obstacles and objections. We are here to support one another on the path to the corner office, the boardroom, the start-up, the remote work opportunity, or the flexible workday. Whichever path you choose, you've earned it and you deserve it.

ABOUT THE AUTHOR

Dr. Katherine Humphreys is currently living in Medellin, Colombia with her British husband, two children, and their recently adopted English Bull Terrier. The family previously lived in a small coastal village in the Dominican Republic. Drawing on their adventures in over 45 countries, Katherine is writing a graphic novel adventure series for young readers.

Prior to her current life as a **worldschool Mom**, Dr. Humphreys was a university administrator. She spent decades managing teams, consulting, presenting at conferences, and serving in professional association roles. She still wears several hats, including managing a real estate portfolio and helping to run the family business. She also serves as a chief logistical officer for all the family's travel and as an 'author mentor' for a publishing company. She seeks joy in exercise, new experiences, and quality time with the people she loves.

www.linkedin.com/in/dr-katherine-humphreys-302453376/

Chapter 9
The Epidural Blinded Me
—Donna Marie Marino

For my children, Lauren and H.L.,
for the love that reordered my life,
and for the legacy that matters more than any title.

"I have found the paradox, that if you love until it hurts, there can be no more hurt, only more love."

— Mother Teresa

I didn't realize how much I wasn't seeing until the moment everything came sharply into focus.

Not because I lacked feeling. I felt deeply about my work, my children, my responsibilities, my life. Feeling was never the problem.

What I didn't see clearly was the cost of operating on autopilot.

For years, I had learned to move fluidly between roles—leader, mother, provider, problem-solver—trusting momentum more than pause. That way of being had served me well.

It was rewarded. It worked.

Until it didn't.

The day my six-year-old daughter was in pain, and I couldn't make it stop, the illusion that all roles could coexist, unchanged, collapsed.

That was the day the epidural blinded me.

A LIFE BUILT ON COMPETENCE

For nearly twenty-five years, my career and I were deeply intertwined. I loved the pace of corporate life—the meetings, the travel, the intellectual challenge, the creative problem-solving. I was trusted with responsibility and recognized for delivery. Opportunity followed opportunity, and I rarely hesitated to step forward.

My identity slowly fused with my competence. I didn't question it. Why would I? I was successful, fulfilled, and very much alive in my work. I felt things intensely and cared deeply—about people, outcomes, and impact.

What mattered most to me in those years was never ego or ambition for its own sake. From early in my life, I had learned that performance was positively rewarded. School was where I felt safe, seen, and valued—a place where I could be fully myself in ways that were not always possible at home. Excellence became a kind of refuge, a language of belonging. Being capable wasn't about standing out; it was about feeling secure.

That conditioning followed me into adulthood. Competence became synonymous with responsibility, reliability, and care. It was how I provided, how I protected, how I made life work—for myself and eventually for my children. When motherhood arrived later than planned, it folded itself into that same rhythm. I believed I could hold everything together through attentiveness, intelligence, and sheer will. I had always found a way.

There had been earlier moments, especially in the fragile years following my divorce, when motherhood pressed itself to the foreground with unmistakable urgency. Moments of terror and devotion that brought me to my knees and asked everything of me. But at that point in my life, newly single and solely responsible for providing for my children, I believed—rightly or wrongly—that stopping was not an option. I endured those moments through resolve and prayer, convincing myself that perseverance was the only responsible choice.

What I could not yet see was how success, itself, can quietly narrow perspective. How effectiveness, reinforced over time, can quietly narrow vision. How auto-pilot doesn't mute feeling so much as it overrides discernment, training us to move forward without stopping to notice what is being missed.

WHEN BIRTH OFFERED A CLUE

When my daughter was born, labor progressed slowly—until suddenly it didn't. Once things moved, they moved fast. An epidural was administered, softening the pain and muting the signals my body would otherwise have sent.

Twenty-two minutes later, she arrived—decisive, spirited, unmistakably herself. When they placed her on my chest, she peed all over me, as if marking me, claiming me as her own. I laughed, unbothered, overwhelmed by love, unaware then of how deeply that moment of water, body, and belonging would echo years later.

That moment changed me forever.

What I did not understand then was how often I would rely on the same kind of numbing—not emotional numbing, but situational masking. A way of blocking sensation just long enough to keep going.

The epidural didn't erase feeling.

It obscured information.

THE DAY EVERYTHING COLLIDED

Years later, on what should have been an ordinary weekday, all of that came rushing back.

The morning required an early start. My son needed to be dropped off at childcare ahead of schedule so I could take my daughter to the hospital for a bladder procedure before heading into a full day of meetings.

The plan was straightforward. Efficient.

Hospital. School drop-off. Back to work.

I had experienced a catheter during childbirth. It wasn't pleasant, but it was manageable.

Standing beside her in that cold hospital room, it suddenly occurred to me what I had missed.

I had been given an epidural.

She had not.

As I held her hand and watched her small body brace itself against fear and pain, something in me recalibrated. This was not a minor inconvenience. This was not something to move past quickly. Her nervous system was overwhelmed; fear had taken up residence in her body.

There was no way I could take her to school afterward.

So I did what seemed reasonable. I took her to work with me.

She loved my office; she had been there many times before. My colleagues adored her. She wrote on my whiteboard, collected candy, and felt special—temporarily distracted from what her body was holding.

Meanwhile, I easily slipped back into my role. Meeting to meeting. Presentation to presentation. I trusted what had always worked.

At one point, I did a quick drive-by to check on her. A colleague quietly let me know how uncomfortable she was.

It was early afternoon. Her bladder was painfully full. She needed to pee—and couldn't. Fear had lodged itself in her body. She was uncomfortable, distressed, and trying very hard to be brave.

I knew this.

And still, I went to one more meeting.

I did what I had been trained to do.

I performed.

As my boss and I walked out of the room, she looked at me and said, "Wow—you really knocked that out of the park."

I said, "Thanks. I don't know how. I pulled it out of my ass." Even as something in me registered the dissonance—how easily the words came, how practiced I was at delivering on demand, and how far that performance now felt from what mattered most.

And then I told her I needed to leave. That my daughter had been struggling all day. That I needed to take her home.

It was two o'clock in the afternoon.

She'd been holding it since before seven o'clock that morning.

I cannot recall a single detail of what I accomplished that day.

But I remember everything that followed.

WHEN SEEING CHANGED EVERYTHING

At home, I tried every practical solution I could think of. Warm water on her hands. Gentle encouragement. Nothing worked. Her body would not release.

So I filled the bathtub.

When the water was warm enough, I climbed in behind her and wrapped my arms around her small body. Skin to skin. Breath to breath.

"I've got you," I whispered. "We're going to do this together."

I rocked her gently and sang the song I had sung to her every morning of her life.

Slowly, her body softened. Hours of holding released. She leaned back into me, finally safe enough to let go.

In that moment, everything became clear.

Not because I felt more—but because I finally saw.

Later, as she rested quietly, cradled in my arms, tears streamed down my face. I held her in a way she couldn't see me, keeping my breath steady, my body calm, whispering soft affirmations into her ear, stroking her hair, letting her know—again and again—that I saw her, that she was brave, that she was safe, while everything inside me gave way. The tears came from a collision of things at once—relief, gratitude for her bravery, and a deep, aching guilt that I had put her through so much that day. I felt upset with myself, almost disgraced in my mothering, as the weight of what I had missed and misjudged settled fully into my body.

Something fundamental had shifted.

STANDING IN THE IN-BETWEEN

In the weeks that followed, I took an honest inventory of my life. I realized that while I could recall every detail of my daughter's fear and relief, I could not remember the substance of the work that had pulled me away from her.

That realization carried weight. When I told my boss that I needed to make a professional change, I said we either needed to reimagine my role in a way that allowed greater flexibility for my children and me, or we needed to begin planning my exit.

She looked at me, almost aghast, and said, "What are you going to do if you're not a Director anymore?"

I tilted my head and, without forethought, said, *"A Director is a title I have—not the woman I am."*

We began planning my exit that day.

On January 31, 2006, as I packed my belongings into the car, a bundle of balloons slipped from my hands and floated upward. I watched them rise until they disappeared.

I felt calm. Clear. Aligned.

I had no plan.

What I did have was the clarity that this moment hadn't come out of nowhere. It arrived after years of quieter reckonings—times when my heart had asked for recalibration long before my life could safely accommodate it. Endurance had carried me through those earlier seasons.

But now, endurance was no longer enough.

But I could finally see.

LEADERSHIP, RECONSIDERED

Clarity brought a powerful reckoning—a shift from embedded beliefs: that leadership does not begin with leading others. It begins with leading ourselves—with the courage to see clearly, and to live from what we see, even when it requires recalibration.

For many women, leadership is lived at the intersection of deep devotion and high responsibility. We carry professional roles that demand excellence, vision, and endurance, while also holding the sacred responsibility of shaping young lives. The tension between mother and executive is not imagined; it is real, persistent, and rarely named honestly.

What matters here is not the specific choice I made, but the clarity that made it unavoidable. Heart-led leadership does not ask all women to choose the same path. Some women stay in corporate roles and lead from integrity within. Some reshape their work. Some step away. Some move in and out across seasons of life. Alignment is not a single decision—it is an ongoing practice of listening and responding honestly to what is true.

What I came to understand is this: when I leave this world, no one will remember the meetings I led, the plans I authored, or the corporate successes I delivered. Those accomplishments mattered in their time—but they were never meant to be the legacy.

What will live on is how I mothered my children. How present I was. How I listened. How I chose them—not perfectly, but faithfully. That influence will echo through their lives, and through the lives they may one day touch, in ways no title ever could.

Heart-led leadership asks us to examine what we are willing to prioritize and what we are willing to release. It asks us to trust discernment over momentum, presence over performance, and long-term legacy over short-term validation. It asks us to honor the reality that seasons change—and that wisdom lies in responding consciously, rather than clinging to what once worked.

Sometimes leadership is not about doing more, but about choosing differently—reordering our lives around what matters most.

Not because we failed.

But because we finally see.

"I have found the paradox, that if you love until it hurts, there can be no more hurt, only more love."

LOVE ENACTED

Heart-Led Leadership for Women Who Refuse to Live Off-Center
A Work of ARMONIA

This chapter marks the moment everything recalibrated.

Love Enacted explores what unfolds after clarity — when presence replaces performance and leadership begins with alignment rather than momentum.

If this chapter resonates, you can join the unfolding here:
www.loveenacted.com
www.linkedin.com/in/donnamarino
www.instagram.com/thedonnamariemarino

ABOUT THE AUTHOR

Donna Marie Marino is a counselor, therapist, and leadership guide whose work centers on helping individuals and organizations live and lead in alignment — mind, body, and spirit. After more than two decades in corporate leadership, she made the courageous decision to step away and recalibrate her life in service of what mattered most.

For nearly twenty years, she has supported women navigating leadership, motherhood, identity, and transition, with a particular focus on heart-led decision-making and embodied clarity. She is the founder of ARMONIA, a counseling and wellness practice rooted in the belief that true leadership emerges when we live in harmony with our values and inner knowing.

Her work invites women to trust discernment over momentum, presence over performance, and to honor their own path, power, and potential — one honest choice at a time.

Chapter 10
Fire That Bitch
—Jean Smarto

Serendipity is a cool thing when it happens in your life. Within the timespan of a week, a woman I respected immensely asked me to write about my career journey, and a second request came from a coaching client at Duquesne University, who was seeking my best career advice. I thought it was a wonderful opportunity to support them both with this chapter. I feel honored to share my story and some lessons learned along the way with you.

My career started as a part-time secretary, and I rose to the level of Director and Chief of Staff in the world's largest investment services company. In addition to earning my MBA, I am an author and coach certified by the ICF (International Coaching Federation). I learned a frequent problem for me, and my clients, is our own negative inner critic. Our inner critic is that bitch inside our head that constantly judges and criticizes us, creating self-doubt. I learned early to fight back and say **Fire that Bitch – Believe in yourself!**

Our inner critic is relentless and often manifests as imposter syndrome. My research found that 75%* of high-performing women report experiencing feelings of imposter syndrome. You are not alone! Imposter syndrome is the persistent feeling of self-doubt and inadequacy that holds you back from reaching your full potential. You may want to seek support from a friend, coach or even a professional, but you can make a positive change today by firing that bitch in your head. You can start by catching your negative inner critic in the act and replacing those thoughts with positive ones. Remind yourself of all your accomplishments. Self-compassion and self-acceptance are also effective tools for reducing internal criticism. Train your inner voice to talk like you would with a trusted friend. **Fire that Bitch - Be your own bestie!**

My career began when I graduated from high school. My parents, following the norms of society, thought it would be best for me to complete a secretarial program because I was a girl! I did two things: one, got a part-time job as a secretary; and two, enrolled in business classes at our local community college. My inner critic told me to become a secretary because that was the best I could hope for in life, but I decided to **Fire that Bitch - Be brave and dream big!**

My part-time secretarial job was at a defense contractor in their Purchasing/Supply Chain Department. My new boss was tough on me. I was given the worst tasks in the department with ridiculous deadlines. This was a common story for women at that time, encountering someone who made the workplace harder than it needed to be. I chose to ignore my inner critic telling me that I wasn't good enough and worked even harder. I succeeded because I chose to **Fire that Bitch - Learn to be resilient and make it your mindset!**

I continued to work hard and rose through the grade levels while finishing my business degree at night, utilizing the company's tuition reimbursement program. During this time, I married and had a child. It was so hard at times. I remember waddling, at almost nine months pregnant, down the university hallway towards a final exam and screaming inside that I should just quit! But I stopped to **Fire that Bitch - Remember, continuous learning is preparing you for what comes next.**

Meanwhile, I continued to excel at work and became a supervisor in the department. This is where I faced a hard lesson. I had expected my female coworkers to support me in my new position, but sadly, things were more difficult. I wonder now if their inner critics were telling them stories that made them judge me harshly for advancing. My inner critic told me I wasn't good enough for the promotion, and that is why the girls weren't supporting me. I learned to **Fire that Bitch - Be confident, maintain professionalism and stay positive.**

In the next few years, I honed my negotiation skills. Being the only woman at the table wasn't easy, but I learned so much from being there. There was one memorable day when several purchasing agents were presenting their latest business justifications to the plant management team for approval. I watched the leadership team decide to give the work to a different supplier, going against the plan that my peer had just presented. This was my first exposure to corporate politics. I will never forget the uncomfortable silence, heads down, and sideways glances when the presenter spoke up with questions. My inner critic was screaming at me and saying I didn't belong at that table. I fought against the voice of my negative inner critic and remembered to **Fire that Bitch – Reading the room is a strategic leadership skill that must be learned.**

The next big event at work caught me completely off guard. The culprit, in a word, recession! I had the longest tenure and was one of just a few with a business degree, and thought I was safe. I was shocked when I was told "off the record" that I would be impacted simply because I was not the sole provider for my family. My inner critic told me I was just a girl and shouldn't have wanted more from my career. I was wounded, but I knew to **Fire that Bitch - Learn to be financially prepared for tough times.**

I wanted a career, so I began my new job search. There was an open Purchasing Manager position for a Fortune 500 manufacturing company near me, so I applied. I got the interview, but the plant manager was reluctant to take a chance on a woman who had never managed an entire department. I used my negotiation skills and creativity to secure a contractor role as their acting manager, while they continued their employment search. After a few months, my bet paid off, and the plant manager realized that I was the right person for the role and hired me. While my inner critic screamed, "I wasn't good enough," I chose to **Fire that Bitch - Know your value and strengths.**

In my new role, I would do a daily walk around the plant floor. During one of my walks, I stopped and chatted with one of the machine operators. He shared how his machine vibrated before it broke down and stopped the line. My instincts told me this was an important finding. At first, my colleagues discounted the significance of the vibration observation, but soon a new process was in place. This change saved crucial downtime and increased the operating efficiency of the line and the plant. Our plant manager was thrilled with the productivity increase. That year our plant won the U.S. Senate Productivity and Quality Award for our state. My inner critic had told me to keep quiet when my colleagues discredited the information. I chose to **Fire that Bitch – Listen to your instincts.**

My life took another turn when my husband accepted a job in a new state. The strain of conflicting priorities was just too much. A move can either make or break a marriage, and this move broke mine. I was now a divorced single parent and needed to up my game to get a better job, so I enrolled in an MBA program and started looking for a new role. I was also starting to worry about the cost of my son's college education. There was an open job at a local university, which was one of the nation's top engineering schools. I knew the university offered free tuition for employees' children after five years of employment. My son was already a junior in high school, and the current program wouldn't help me. I put my negotiator training to work again. After I nailed the interview, I negotiated my salary, knowing what I really wanted was the free tuition for my son and got it. When my inner critic told me I couldn't get what I wanted, I chose to **Fire that Bitch - Take a risk and don't be afraid to ask for what you want!**

I worked at the University while my son completed his degree in engineering. I advanced and continued to take classes. My salary was a bit low for the market, but I will forever feel grateful for my son's free tuition. At the university, a new CFO was in place and reorganization was underway. I had been confidentially alerted that my team was going to be laid off. I faced a crisis again. What should I say or not say? I decided to give my director a heads-up so he could be prepared for what was going to happen and trusted him to keep my confidence. My decision to tell him ended badly for us both, but it also taught me how important it is to stay true to my core values. I learned that loyalty is a core value to me in my personal relationships and the danger of letting my personal feelings affect my business decisions. My inner critic told me I had made a big mistake. I decided to **Fire That Bitch – Stay true to your core values even when it is hard.**

My next role was in financial services where I was starting over again as a negotiator. Shortly after I joined the company, a leadership change happened. I was ready to ask for more responsibility. The new leader was a woman. She was interviewing everyone who expressed an interest in being on her new leadership team. She was tough! After the interview, the new CPO, Chief Procurement Officer, looked me in the eye and told me that I didn't have what was needed to be on her team. I was devastated but I didn't stop to listen to my inner critic. I immediately told her I was confident that I could prove I had the skills, if given the opportunity. Shortly after, I was assigned to negotiate the contract with the consulting firm leading the transformation effort. Within a year of her hiring, I was given the opportunity to be the internal program manager for the project. I took on this new role with a strong conviction to prove to her that I was competent and deserved her trust. I enjoyed working for her and further advanced the following year to the position of Chief of Staff. It was a tough time with a lot of travel but a rewarding phase in my career. My inner critic wanted to crush me and say I wasn't good enough to perform at this new level. I am so proud that I remembered to **Fire that Bitch - Stand up and advocate for yourself!**

There were so many lessons learned in my new leadership position. I learned that an executive's time is extremely limited and that I needed to remember three things: 1) respect their time and be prompt, 2) speak clearly and concisely, and 3) always offer solutions. I knew that my main responsibility was to make her job easier. I also learned that leaders hate surprises and they want and need you to watch out for them. I admit that I fell into the trap of being a perfectionist and hard to please. This tendency frequently happens when you are faced with more responsibility and demands for your time. The additional pressure and multiple expectations created stress and bad behavior that I needed to learn to keep in check. My inner critic was out of control on many days, but I learned to **Fire the Bitch – Focus on the task at hand and do great work.**

This was also when I learned a great deal about organizational behavior from watching the team's interactions. I learned that people are always communicating, even when we are silent. I came to understand that people will naturally think first about how an event, action or situation will impact them. A notable example was when I was following the CPO down the office hallway. When she failed to acknowledge people as she passed, I saw worry appear on their faces. We all have natural psychological defense mechanisms to protect ourselves from perceived threats. The team members' faces reflected their fear the CPO would eliminate their role, since she hadn't acknowledged them. However, the CPO was just extremely busy and thinking about the next demand from the senior management team. I learned that I am not the only one with a negative inner critic and the importance of communication. I learned when my inner critic becomes too self-focused to **Fire that Bitch – Be present and connect with others to build important relationships.**

I had a few other opportunities open-up for me during this time. I was asked to teach in the Leaders as Teachers program at work. I also applied and was accepted into the Finance Leadership Development Program. From the program, I learned the importance of setting SMART (specific, measurable, achievable, relevant and time-bound) goals. These goals should only be established for what truly matters and can be measured. My inner critic told me I wasn't special enough for this additional training, but I knew to quickly **Fire that Bitch – Document your personal and professional goals/priorities and your accomplishments.**

As I progressed through my career, I saw the cycle of corporate leadership change happening more frequently. After reading the latest annual report, my instincts told me to be ready for another regime change and to find a safer position in the organization. I was aware that new senior executives often bring with them their trusted leadership team members. So, I interviewed for an embedded team leadership role. The stress in the department was palpable. Soon after this leadership change occurred, my prior leader's departure was not a surprise. I knew that her core values would prevent her from modeling the company's new incoming culture. My inner critic told me to be fearful of change, but I knew to **Fire that Bitch - Change is the only constant (adapt or get left behind).**

I focused on my new team; it performed well and saved the organization approximately $500M. The key to my leadership style was empathy. I knew the pitfalls of micro-management; a good manager must accept and understand that employees may have a different approach to achieving the desired outcome. I also learned that part of my role was to be their heat shield against the company's new culture. As a leader and manager, I took seriously my role to provide an environment for continuous learning and improvement for my team. I discovered how much I personally enjoyed coaching individuals to grow and become better versions of themselves. My inner critic was worried about what other people might say about me, but I chose to **Fire that Bitch - Find a mentor or coach to help you grow; then become one for someone else!**

Next, things got even tougher. We would need to do more with less and layoffs were imminent. I was told to find someone on my team and rate them as "below expectations" on their next review. By the numbers, my team was the highest functioning team in the department. My only choice was to give the rating or I would get it. Every member of my team had met their goals, and I couldn't comply with this direction in good conscience, so I made my choice to take it instead. My bonus was reduced by 25%, but I slept well at night. My inner critic screamed at me for being so foolish and not watching out for myself. I knew to **Fire that Bitch – It will always be easier to live with loss than regret doing what is right.**

My career priorities were beginning to shift. My mother's health was failing, and I knew the time left was limited. I was juggling both work and my caregiver responsibilities and feeling like I was failing at both. It was a very difficult time in my life. After she passed, my fulfillment and purpose could no longer be found at work. I had every symptom of burnout and needed to find a new path. I remembered how much I loved helping people to be their best, so I enrolled in an evening/weekend professional coach certification program at Duquesne University to ignite a spark in me again. For the same reason I loved managing others, I love coaching and helping others to be their best. My inner critic warned me that I might fail if I tried to do something new, but I decided to **Fire that Bitch - Be open to finding a new path at any age.**

Below is a summary of all the lessons I have learned from firing my bitchy inner critic! I am thankful for all the growth she inspired along the way.

1. Believe in yourself.
2. Be your own bestie.
3. Be brave and dream big.
4. Learn to be resilient and make it your mindset.
5. Remember continuous learning is preparing you for what comes next.
6. Be confident, maintain professionalism and stay positive.
7. Reading the room is a strategic leadership skill that must be learned.
8. Learn to be financially prepared for tough times.
9. Know your value and strengths.
10. Listen to your instincts.
11. Take a risk and don't be afraid to ask for what you want.
12. Stay true to your core values even when it is hard.
13. Stand up and advocate for yourself!
14. Focus on the task at hand and do great work.
15. Be present and connect with others to build important relationships.
16. Document your goals and accomplishments.

17. Change is the only constant (adapt or get left behind).
18. Find a mentor or coach to help you grow; then become one for someone else!
19. It will always be easier to live with loss than regret doing what is right.
20. Be open to finding a new path at any age.

Isn't it time to fire your bitch too?

Sources for Additional Learning:

- *KPMG Study Finds 75% Of Female Executives Across Industries Have Experienced Imposter Syndrome In Their Careers
- Understanding the Inner Critic | Psychology Today
- "How to Silence the Inner Critic: A Guide to Self-Compassion" | Brene Brown |

ABOUT THE AUTHOR

Jean Smarto is an author, speaker, and ICF-certified professional coach with over 30 years of experience in corporate America. During her career, Jean achieved the role of Director and Chief of Staff at the world's largest investment services company. She is a seasoned business leader who has led global teams in complex, cross-cultural environments. She coaches students in the University of Pittsburgh's MBA program and Duquesne University's Supply Chain Program. Jean is also the author of the children's book *My Character Check*, which helps parents and children engage in meaningful conversations about character, values, and learning from mistakes to become better tomorrow. My Character Check inspires readers to live by their core values. She is currently working on her next children's book, designed to equip kids with practical steps for resolving conflict in healthy and constructive ways.

Jean Smarto, MBA, ACC
www.mycharactercheck.com
www.linkedin.com/in/jsmarto
www.instagram.com/my_character_check

Chapter 11
Abandoning the Script
—Michelle McCartney

Something was wrong. I wasn't sure what it was, but during every contraction, I could feel it… Before I began verbally assaulting my entire nursing staff and husband, something I had once been taught was now plaguing me.

Birth didn't have to be painful.

If you're a mother, you're probably rolling your eyes or even getting a giggle out of that one. Maybe, just maybe, you're the type of woman who identifies strongly with that statement. After having 4 kids, I am rolling my eyes. When I was pregnant with my first, my midwife had taught me the concept of painless childbirth. It was predicated upon the idea that many cultures around the world birth completely pain-free simply because their society never normalized painful births.

I went into my first birthing experience fully expecting it to hurt, but not be scream-worthy. After all, other cultures didn't scream when they gave birth… right?

Well… I started screaming.

Before we start assuming that the midwifery clinic was negligent or teaching pseudoscience, the actual facts around what they taught were true!

There are cultures that birth painlessly, and there are societies that honor birth as a natural process instead of showcasing it from a place of pain and fear. The natural conclusion that people could just mindset their way into a painless birth, however, was what got me.

The moment that I felt the strong surge overcome my body was the moment that I assumed something must be wrong. It wasn't supposed to feel this way. It wasn't supposed to be THIS painful. I was supposed to be able to endure and tolerate this, not want to bulldoze every single person around me. Our bodies were designed for this, right?

I became deeply afraid that my body couldn't do what it was designed to do.

After twenty-two hours, I finally fell into my husband's arms, sobbing and confided that I wanted the epidural. I didn't want to be a "bad mom" by drugging myself and our child. After some time elapsed, even though time was an illusion at this point, the nurses and my husband convinced me that getting the epidural was not a sign of being a bad mother, but rather that I just needed a little extra help. I got the epidural, took a two-hour nap, and immediately woke up to the feeling of a balloon bursting inside my pelvis. That gush of water indicated that it was "go time." After two and a half hours of pushing and some assistance from a vacuum, my daughter was born.

I will *never* get the chance to redo this experience.

When I had my second child, I knew what to expect. I knew that it was okay for it to be painful. I knew that every woman gets to a place where they feel like they can't do it anymore and that they usually meet their baby shortly after that point. I knew that I had given birth before. I knew that my husband would support me.

I used a different midwifery practice and had a deeply empowering unmedicated homebirth. One that showed me what I was capable of. One where I surrendered to the flow of birth, died, went to heaven to collect my child, and came back a completely new woman. One where my screams turned into a roar. One that transformed the way I view everything.

Most importantly, it showed me that a woman's strength is in her soft surrender.

The surrender of comfort, the surrender of control, and the surrender of expectations.

What I didn't understand then was that I hadn't failed my body during my first birth; I had failed myself by believing someone else's definition of what the "right" way to do something was.

I later went on to give birth to two more children, a daughter who broke the record as the biggest baby our midwives had ever delivered (12lb 5oz in an unmedicated homebirth), and then a baby boy who flipped breech towards the end of my pregnancy, resulting in a last-minute pivot to a cesarean.

Everyone will give you an opinion about birth, success, or how to live a worthy life as a woman. Although they're beautiful and well-intentioned, they work for *someone else.*

I didn't misunderstand the midwives. Their teachings weren't wrong. They just weren't right for *me,* and they just weren't right for *right now.*

And that distinction, between understanding a vision and surrendering to your own, would take me years to fully grasp.

Eventually, I would recognize that same theme in mom's groups, business networking, and just about every space where people come together to "give each other advice." I felt the subtle pressure to expand faster, to want more, to endure discomfort quietly and to prove strength by tolerating pain that wasn't mine to carry.

For seven years, I navigated the tides of bringing new children into this world, raising them, and going through it all over again. Through all of this, I was also pushing through creating and growing businesses to support the life that I had always envisioned for my family.

When we go back to the beginning, I realize that I knew deep in my soul that I HAD to be home with my children. My husband shared this vision with me, but our bank account did not. While my husband worked to continuously get promotion after promotion, his paycheck just wasn't keeping up.

We had to figure something out, so we decided that I would start a business to bring in some extra income while raising our children.

Cue the nervous laughter…

How does a mom navigate pregnancies, maternity leaves, and postpartum while being a solo entrepreneur? How does a mom do sales calls with her kids in the same room as her? How does a mom cook everything from scratch, keep the house spotless, homeschool, do bathtime, look flawless, and grow a business?

It all felt impossible.

I started with something small. What is something that I *can* do?

While scrolling through YouTube one day, I saw a video that would change my life forever. A video talking about how bookkeeping was the perfect business for a stay-at-home mom to start! It was relatively easy to learn; you didn't have to spend tons of time on camera or on calls, and you could do it whenever you wanted, so working during nap time was possible.

How hard can this be?

I purchased a few bookkeeping-for-dummies books and got to reading. Within a month, I had finished 5 different bookkeeping books and drawn up comprehensive notes. I had a QuickBooks Online account and had even learned the software.

Now, all I needed was a client.

I spent the next 5 months posting in every business group I could find on Facebook, I sent messages to everybody I knew and let them know that I was just getting started and was looking for someone I could work with for free for a few months to get my feet wet.

Then, someone bit!

"Oh yeah! My husband owns a construction company and is looking for a new bookkeeper!"

And that was it. I worked for this construction company, and after two months of free work, they hired me.

I couldn't believe it! Someone was paying ME to keep track of their books, and I was doing it during nap times! Then, I got another client.

I joined a few local networking groups and took my daughter with me so I wouldn't miss out.

I was the only attendee who showed up with a baby, but everyone respected it. I overheard a couple of colleagues in our group talking about me and labeled me as a *real hustler*.

Honestly, I was proud. I was doing all the right things. I was networking, getting new clients, and growing the business. I was making more money and having an actual impact on our family.

When I got pregnant with our second child. I started getting tired easier and groggier. My brain fog seemed to be overtaking me, and the monotony of entrepreneurship kicked in.

It was the same thing day in and day out, and I didn't even like what I was doing. In fact, logging into QuickBooks was my least favorite part of my day.

I began to feel trapped inside the jail that I had built around myself in the name of "freedom."

After all, that's what this was supposed to be, right? Financial freedom, time freedom, and freedom to live life on my terms. Except now my schedule was dictated by clients' schedules, deadlines, nap times, and waiting to work until my husband was home.

Then, a business coach told me that if I was too busy to accept new work, then it was time to hire employees. So, I hired people whom I knew who were going through financial struggles. I wanted to help them get their feet back on the ground. I trained them and passed off work to them and figured "problem solved."

Now I can spend more time with my kids again and not have to worry about anything.

Five months later, I found myself in the middle of a miscarriage and getting a letter in the mail from the state that I had to appear in court with this employee. Within the next few months, I was out thousands of dollars and all of my clients.

I was forced with the decision to either rebuild my business or close it down and do something else.

I couldn't fathom going back to actually doing all of the bookkeeping, so I chose to close down and re-group.

I was completely and utterly embarrassed. How could I end up in this situation? I thought I was too smart for this. I thought I was too organized and strategic to end up in this moment. Then, I made a post on Facebook where twenty or thirty business owners reached out to me privately with solidarity. They had been in this situation before, and, in fact, I now know that this is just the price so many pay for growth.

My story is not unique, and I felt so beaten up and discouraged because of it. The more impactful you are in life, the more risk you take on. Until you have the knowledge, experience, and team to handle some of those risks, things like this just happen.

Despite these deep lessons, I managed to do the same thing all over again. After the bookkeeping business, I started a marketing agency. I figured that if I was going to be in the entrepreneurial world, then learning marketing would be important, no matter what I decided to do. So, I started a social media management agency that ultimately grew to a full-fledged marketing agency that did logo design, branding, web design, email marketing, SEO, and more.

Years into it, I made the same mistake. I was so quick to hire that I wasn't set up properly for it, hired the wrong people, and the whole business crumbled when I was giving birth to my fourth child.

I learned to stop forcing growth. Stop trying to fit a specific image of success. Stop trying to get to an end result.

Instead, enjoy the journey, surrender to the situation, and smell the damn roses.

I spent so much time trying to make as much money as fast as possible so that I could get the bigger car, have the bigger home, and enjoy the nicer stuff. I spent so long rushing for success, which ultimately stopped me from having the success that I wanted.

What I was building wasn't sustainable. It was trying to build a skyscraper on the foundation of a shed (and all in the name of proving to others that I could find a way to bring in good money while being a stay-at-home mom).

In all honesty, slowing down and being more intentional still isn't easy for me. I'm naturally a very ambitious person and aim big, but my approach to it is now totally different. Now, I just work on the end result I'm helping my clients accomplish, not my own end result.

Now, I take the time to adequately test, get feedback, and grow. Slowly but intentionally.

Women are not suffering because they aren't strong enough; they're suffering because they are living according to expectations that were never theirs. Something changes, though, when we choose to surrender instead.

Surrender isn't passivity, giving up, or a lack of ambition. It requires brutal honesty, self-trust, and the willingness to disappoint others.

When I embraced surrendering, I grew stronger in listening instead of pushing, responding instead of reacting, and honoring different seasons of life instead of trying to hit deadlines. Just because something was possible didn't mean it was required of me. That felt really hard to reconcile, so let me say it again. *Just because something was possible didn't mean it was required of me.*

As women, we have unique strengths and characteristics that define how we shape the world. While men hunt, gather, and fight, women listen, observe, and take silent action. Women are softer and more supportive in nature, often leading us to take roles that support the world rather than asserting ourselves into it. The more we try to manifest masculine natures into our feminine existence, the more we burn out.

Over time, I learned to drop everyone's expectations. I learned that it's okay if things take longer than they're supposed to. I learned that the bigger the dream and ambition, the longer it'll take to build the foundation. I learned that you can live a completely intentional life (and that it's okay if it takes you time to figure out what that looks like). I learned that my kids get more from having a happy and well-rounded mom instead of one who is always hustling on a computer trying to scale faster than she can manage.

This is the heart of everything that I do now. I spend my days homeschooling my 4 small children, baking bread at home in an apron and oven mitts, snuggling with my fluffy Maine Coon, and hopping onto coaching calls to help other moms build a business that aligns with their values, impact, and doesn't take them away from their families.

The most powerful decision I've ever made wasn't to grow faster, work harder, or endure more.

It was to surrender to the life I was actually meant to live.

A life that was slow, intentional, and beautifully sustainable. A life that allowed me to grow at my own pace instead of forcing growth to try and prove something to a society and culture that doesn't care about me. A life that, in its own silent and soft way, was the most rebellious thing I could cultivate. A life that told the world that a woman doesn't have to choose between family or career. A life that actually balances softness without having to step into the masculine energy of forced growth. A life that didn't expect me to choose between family or career. A life that didn't make me abandon what truly matters.

If you feel like you're failing, it might be time to slow down. Breathe deeply, and look for that deep creative energy inside of you. What are you meant to do with your life? Who are you meant to be? What kind of impact do you want to have on the world? Is it a system or organization you build, or is it a person you raise? Is it both?

When you take the time to truly discover who you are, you can write the script for your own life. You can surrender to the pain that comes with growth and change. You can withstand the metamorphosis of coming out of the cocoon.

When you surrender, you stop fighting. You give in and finally soften. In that softening is where you'll heal, where you'll gain clarity, and where the vision for your life will be revealed.

So, when you pick up the pen, what script are you writing for your life?

~

Join the Mompreneur Club:

ABOUT THE AUTHOR

Michelle McCartney is a Christian wife, homeschooling mother of four, entrepreneur, and lifelong learner who believes growth is essential.

With a newborn in her arms, Michelle taught herself bookkeeping and built a business during nap times. Over seven years, she grew a bookkeeping firm, launched a marketing agency, navigated setbacks, and rebuilt more than once. Along the way, she learned that real strength isn't found in forcing expansion, but in building a life and business aligned with your deepest convictions.

Today, Michelle coaches mothers who feel called to be present at home yet refuse to abandon their gifts and earning potential. Through her Mompreneur Club, she helps women design sustainable businesses that support their families without consuming them.

When she's not coaching, Michelle is homeschooling her children, baking from scratch, planning her family's next adventure, or snuggling her oversized orange Maine Coon. She believes women are strongest when they lead from conviction rather than comparison and that the fastest way to growth is through entrepreneurship and motherhood, so might as well do both.

Chapter 12
The Un-Abandonable Mission
—Asya Dimitrova

I have always seen connections, everywhere, between everything. I thought everyone else could do that, too. I could not imagine another way of viewing life, but quickly learned that this made me a strange one - "too intense" and "too much" for people to handle.

My earliest memory of being in danger for seeing the world differently happened in a house full of flowers and tears. I was four.

My grandmother's friend had passed away. It was inappropriate for a child to be at a funeral, but there was no one else to watch me, so she took me to the little house and left me in the beautifully blossoming garden while she went inside to pay her respects. I was fascinated by the strange, quiet behaviour of the adults, who walked gloomily into the house and emerged clutching handkerchiefs, crying. I had to know what was happening.

I wriggled my way amongst the adults dressed in black, to the centre of the room, where a big wooden box was set on the kitchen table. Someone kindly lifted me to peek into the coffin. What I saw wasn't scary or sad; it was simply a shell, like a doll left behind. The warm feeling of the lovely lady she used to be - wasn't there. Yet all around me, adults were crying with a deep sorrow that, to my four-year-old mind, didn't match the emptiness in the box.

When my grandmother spotted me, I saw disapproval explode behind her eyes. I had crossed a line. She carried me back to the garden, and then, unexpectedly, hugged me, her own tears falling as she murmured, "Oh, my poor little girl..." Other mourners pouring out from the house surrounded us, patting my head, assuming I was horrified, predicting an unhinged future for me.

The thing was that more than 40 years ago, in rural Bulgaria, strangeness was dangerous. The differently-abled kids (physically or mentally) were taken away from their families and locked in institutions. Parents of "weird" kids were scared out of their minds and would hurry to discipline them into "normality" before the white coats came knocking on their door.

Back in the dead lady's garden, I was trying to tell them what I had seen, or rather, what I hadn't. But as I spoke, I saw a wall of stern, calculating eyes, a refusal to hear anything that disturbed their story. They were looking for a sign in me, was I "a strange one"? That day, I learned a lesson that would shape the next forty years of my life: my perceptions and others' reality were two different things, and theirs was the one that mattered. My little frightened self then decided to stop talking to adults for a very long time.

My older cousin, Tony, was the one who helped me bridge the two realities. We talked a lot, and he tried to explain the adult world to me. Adults had certain ways of being, he said, and they like things to be "normal". If I disturbed them, they would get uneasy, angry, or confused. "And confused people," he told me, "turn nasty very quickly. They'll try to 'help' you to get back to normal. But if you give them what they expect, they will leave you be."

Growing up with the idea that there were two different worlds and I wasn't broken made all the difference (which I now know is not an option for many children). Learning the adults' rules became my special interest. I spent years in deep focus, memorising society's scripts so I could give adults what they needed to see from me in order to make them feel safe, which in turn allowed me to be myself when I was alone.

This understanding helped, but it created a new challenge: I had to constantly watch myself, and it was easy to slip up. I remember a time, as a teenager, when a girl was bullying me relentlessly. My mind, in its strange way, didn't see what all the other kids thought as cruel anger; I could see the patterns behind it, the sadness and violence in her family, the loneliness she was fighting. It was her secret, but everything in her being was telling me a story: the way she held herself, the way she breathed or stared at things, the way her voice sounded, and her choices of words - I could read it like a book. Until one day, she went too far. I turned, and before I could stop myself, in a low, deliberate voice, I described her own life back to her as I saw it in my head. I didn't mean it as an attack, but as a way of saying, "I see you. Back off!"

The effect was immediate. She crumpled to the ground sobbing, overcome with a panic I hadn't intended. A feeling of power washed over me like a cold shock. I realised my words, my way of seeing, could have a profound and unintended impact. It was a clumsy, painful lesson in responsibility that comes with that kind of perception. After that day, I became even more careful. My insights did not feel like power but a danger that needed to be contained.

For years, that containment was my normal. The exhaustion of constantly diminishing myself, calculating what was expected of me, of holding back the truest parts of my thoughts just to keep the peace, started seeping into everything. It made me feel tired and small. As I went through my life, I built a sense of normalcy for myself: started a company, ran an organization in Spain, and found myself a single parent in the UK. Always with that awkward feeling of a fish trying to fly. I was in the right world, but in the wrong environment.

The change began where I least expected it - I took a job in autism care that I knew nothing about. As I said, any strangeness was erased from society when I was growing up, and nobody would talk about it. On my first day, I was sent to work alone with a young man known for being volatile. The moment I entered his room, it felt like walking into a water tank. The air was thick, heavily saturated with his presence. I sensed his attention scanning me, and in my scared mind, unsettling images flashed from what I've read in his case notes. He moved - I saw his hand clench, I gasped and froze, and he got ready to pounce. In the blinding darkness of my own panic, it hit me: my mind was the problem. My dread was infecting his space. He was reacting to my reactions.

I closed my eyes, took a breath, and changed the image in my head: a mountain trail, blue skies, the buzz of bees, ahh… peace. When I exhaled and opened my eyes, he had sunk back into the sofa, lifting his arms as if to catch the bees I had imagined. He smiled to himself and turned on the TV. I stood there speechless. What had just happened? I knew I had touched something real, like a different set of physics from another person's world, rules no one had ever spoken about. It wasn't about controlling him; it was about managing myself. That was the first time my sensitivity felt less like a problem and more like a useful skill. I had just found what my mind was designed to do.

This experience unlocked everything. I learned that by regulating my own internal states, I could create a space where others could feel safe. When I tried to share these ideas at work, the response was kind but clear: without formal qualifications, my insights were just anecdotes. I did not see this as a rejection but as a clarification. If I could not unsee the patterns and reasons behind strange behaviours, and if I could not teach others what I knew for lack of a diploma, then I had to get one.

For weeks and months, I wrestled with myself. Years of 'being raised right' screamed in my head. I should know my place, stick to the work I had, raise my children, and hope one day they would do better than me. Maybe someone smarter, more educated, will discover that some of what I have glimpsed is possible, and maybe, in the future, science will make it okay. But I couldn't sleep, I couldn't concentrate on the daily tasks, I couldn't stop seeing the patterns of the system in my head applied everywhere – from how traffic could be better organised to people's unconscious glances at strangers on the bus. The ability to connect anything to anything was emerging from the shadows and breaking its chains.

This turmoil was eating me up; I was becoming profoundly unhappy with the world. I loved my work; autistic children would do the most bizarre things that would make sense to me - I could see how their logic worked, and what could make things better. But I was infuriated that they needed so many things changed, but science was not moving fast enough to make a difference in their lives, now. Their parents were struggling every day, their teachers, my colleagues - it felt like we were on our own. So, at 44, I decided to go back to university and accelerate my discoveries. The passive misery of pretending was over. The lonely struggles to survive, hiding my own "strangeness," had become a mission to learn how to use it.

That decision, like the one to keep myself hidden, changed everything but in reverse. The moment I committed to pursuing a degree in neuroscience, a new kind of energy flowed into my life. I signed up against all the hushed comments and raised eyebrows about "going back to school at my age". The work was harder than anything I'd ever done, and I still wasn't sleeping, but for the first time, it wasn't draining; it was energising. I could not get enough of reading and connecting more dots, confirming that what I was already working with had real grounding. I found a new special interest.

By following the thread of my own true curiosity, my whole world began to align. Having so much to say about what my work with the autistic children had taught me, I applied to speak at the Autism Show. The organizer, intrigued and blunt, warned me that my ideas were vulnerable without credentials. "Publish something," he said. So, in three months, I wrote a book that I sold after my talks. It was a raw, rushed attempt at putting ideas to paper, but autistic people came to me saying I had given words to their reality and asking if those ideas had been researched anywhere.

That got me thinking about research, and I started digging through academic papers to see what had been discovered to answer my questions, but everything I found was fragmented, partial, and unclear. My journey led me to King's College London into a cutting-edge Master's program, and for the first time, I was in an environment where my "weird" questions were the right questions. My obsessive need to connect disparate fields was not a flaw; it was the very definition of interdisciplinary science.

It felt like coming home to a place I never knew I longed for, and I found the courage to present my ideas to a world-class professor who did not dismiss them as "strange". She read them, she challenged them, she helped me forge them into something stronger. She became my supervisor, and I am now researching the very world that I spent most of my life trying to cut out of myself. Starting my own research gave my once-feared abilities a purpose and a goal; I was fueled by an energy and drive I never thought was possible.

The roaring battle in my mind between connecting patterns and keeping quiet about them is gone now. That energy is channelled into figuring out the best ways to prove what I see, not delete it. I've learned that my path isn't to be an expert with all the answers. It's to be a kind guide or an investigator of the wonderful neurodivergent inner worlds that many people cannot see. For them, I wish to scientifically map the patterns and figure out the physics of those vastly mesmerising neurodivergent perceptions. This work is not about declaring one way right and another wrong, but showing others how they can navigate their own unique territory, or that of their children, safely and insightfully.

I do not know what my future holds, but I know it is not about arriving at a final destination of some great, glorious illumination. To me, success and self-leadership are the daily, un-abandonable practice of catching that faint, internal thread that tells you when you are out of sync with yourself, and the courage to follow it, even when it leads you away from the crowd and common scripts.

This journey has taught me that our greatest perceived weaknesses are often clues pointing to the raw material of our sacred gifts. The way I see it, these talents are not meant for us, personally; that would be too selfish. They are like letters sent to humanity by the universe, passing through us but addressed to others. We are just the mail carriers, and it would be a crime to keep for ourselves the parcels we were meant to deliver. Think about it; what if others are keeping to themselves what you need to progress in your life, by not sharing your true powers?

If you are a woman or a man who has ever felt like you were "too much" or "too intense," my story is a testimony to a simple truth: the world doesn't need you to fit in. It needs you to be your fullest, most authentic self. Your strangeness is not a weakness; it's the clue to your unique talents, and your only job is to understand them and use them for good.

ABOUT THE AUTHOR

Asya Dimitrova is a researcher at King's College London's Institute of Psychiatry, Psychology & Neuroscience (IoPPN), where she is developing a new, systemic understanding of the mind-body interface in neurodiversity. Her 'Atypical Allostasis' model reframes autism not as a disorder, but as a different, high-performance biological operating system.

A mother of four neurodivergent children, her work is deeply informed by both lived experience and a decade of direct support for the neurodivergent community. She is the author of *'Talento Autismo' (Spanish edition)*, has presented her work at international conferences, and is the creator of the "Hidden Genius Within" course for parents and professionals.

Her long-term mission is to establish a research institute dedicated to a new social framework where neurodivergent talents are cultivated as a vital part of humanity's evolution. Aware that one person cannot build a cathedral alone, she is on a path to bring together the brilliant, resonant minds needed to lay the foundations for a more hopeful future.

www.linkedin.com/in/asya-dimitrova-a14577139
HiddenGenius.co.uk
asya.dimitrova@kcl.ac.uk
connect@hiddengenius.co.uk

Chapter 13
The Power of Saying Yes
—Tiffany Harris

"Let's get ready to say YES!" I thought to myself on a Friday morning in June 2023. I was in the back corner of a conference room, mentally running through my slides for my workshop on the "Power of Saying Yes" at Purdue University's annual Women's Conference. The room was softly lit with recessed lights and the stream of the mid-morning sunlight coming from the east-facing window. Attendees entered the room, and the buzz of their conversations was comforting as they seemed engaged and ready for my presentation. I was feeling rested, refreshed, and sharp. I moved from the back of the room to the front, smiling and nodding along the way to ladies I met the day before during the first day of the conference. Although I was nervous, I was encouraged by the friendly faces of ladies who looked excited to be attending my workshop. In the next hour, I would share my vision of how saying 'Yes' opened doors for me and led to personal and professional success. My intention was to inspire others to feel brave while navigating their life's journey, and that it could all happen with one simple word, "Yes." I arrived at the front of the room and worked with the IT professional to set up my laptop for the presentation. When the presentation was ready, a member of the Conference committee stepped to the podium to introduce me. I closed my eyes and silently prayed, "May the words out of my mouth and the meditations of my heart, be acceptable in thine sight." I stilled myself until I heard the end of my introduction, walked to the podium and started my presentation. This was a message that I spent over twenty years living. In the beginning, I wasn't even aware that I was living this mantra. My "Yes" was more out of requirement or curiosity rather than ego or a higher purpose. Saying "Yes" always seemed to land me one step closer to where I needed to be or should be. However, as I looked over this room of women, I couldn't help but think about how far I had come in twenty-two years since leaving this school with a Master's in Business Administration (MBA).

In May 2001, at twenty-two years old, I left Purdue University with an MBA and no job. No big fancy offer was provided to me. No invite into a prestigious leadership development program. No promise of a career for the adult life I always imagined. I felt shame and embarrassment. I felt like a failure and a fraud. I was leaving a prestigious master's program without a job and was headed to my mother's house in Cleveland, Ohio. Since I was twelve years old, all I wanted to be was a grown-up. I set a plan for myself that I had seen through. I graduated high school in three years, a bachelor's degree in four years, and now I had an MBA at an age where many, if not most, of my peers were still pursuing their Bachelor's degree.

For the first time, I felt untethered and unsure of myself. In my dreams of being an adult, joblessness was not part of the vision. I was unprepared for how to handle the complex emotions I was feeling. I didn't dare share these feelings with my mom or family members who supported me along the way. I didn't even say the words to myself - shame, embarrassment, FAILURE. However, not saying the words out loud to myself or others didn't minimize the weight of those feelings. The residue of those deep-seated feelings took root and sprouted inside me. I was starting adulthood with success and failure happening at the same time. It would be years before I would unearth the tangled mess of what those feelings of shame and embarrassment did in my head and heart. I walked around for years feeling like a fraud because I defined one moment of what felt like failure as an indictment of who I was. Since I felt like a failure, I assumed I would be judged as a failure. I couldn't trust myself, and I didn't trust others for fear of absorbing their judgment.

While in Cleveland, Ohio, living with my mother and younger brother, I had a few job leads, but the prospects were bleak. Within a couple of weeks, those leads were 'Nos'. Unexpectedly, a call came in from the aerospace company I interned with the summer before regarding an Analyst position. While I enjoyed the internship, I didn't envision myself working there. The Analyst position didn't sound like something I would enjoy or perform well at. "Was I setting myself up for another failure?" I wondered. After completing the in-person interview, I half-hoped that I wouldn't get the position. I didn't graduate with a clear vision of the ideal job. Yet I knew, based on my experiences with workbooks and worksheets, that working behind a computer screen in Excel spreadsheets wasn't a dream job situation. Ultimately, I was extended an offer for a fair salary with relocation and a small signing bonus. Without any other prospects in sight, I ruefully accepted the position without fanfare or excitement. I told no one other than my mother and sister about the new job. I moved to Indianapolis, Indiana, and proceeded to spend the next five years in-and-out of a depressive funk.

Adulting was tough. The guardrails of college were off, and I felt thrust into the wilderness of figuring out what my life would look like. My support system of family members seemed to be splintering at the seams as they dealt with individual and family difficulties. When I moved to Indianapolis, I knew less than a handful of people whom I would classify as 'associates'. Admittedly, I also hid. I didn't share my feelings of shame with anyone, and I only shared my misery with my mother and sister. They encouraged me, but I was rudderless. I was defeated.

After a couple of months of complaining and bemoaning my circumstances, I started to get on my own nerves. I started looking for opportunities to socialize and make friends. Next, I found a volunteer opportunity with the Big Brothers, Big Sisters organization for a daytime program where I would meet with a student at a local elementary school. This two-hour commitment, where I could be a hero in someone's day with McDonald's and a listening ear, allowed me to focus on someone other than myself. I also started joyful routines; morning coffee at Starbucks, a bi-weekly hair appointment and leaning into my faith. I joined a church, attended services on Sunday and during the week. I looked for signs anywhere I could that would signal encouragement for my spirit. One morning, as I dragged myself to work, I stopped for my morning coffee and quite literally ran into Isiah Thomas, then the coach for the Indianapolis Pacers basketball team. The interaction was brief, but I felt lighter and more intentional in that moment. I headed into work that morning and the mornings after, looking forward to what else could happen as part of my early morning coffee pick-ups. Moments like this encouraged me to step further out of my comfort zone. I started socializing within my work group, going out for a day of golfing and lunching with co-workers on Fridays. Although these activities offered bright spots throughout the weeks and months, most days still felt bleak and depressing.

While my first position was in fact not a fit for the way I worked best, it only lasted six-months. As the project faced a downturn, it looked like I was going to be laid off along with other teammates. However, I moved into their engineering business development department, where I was responsible for supporting their college engineering cooperative education program. This program supported about sixty students working on-site for internship-type job rotations with the ultimate goal of joining the company once they graduated with an engineering degree. I started this new role without any clear guardrails of my role. However, I instinctively started the work of improving processes and operational inefficiencies. I was soon ingratiated into the Human Resources department, teams of engineering managers, and the students who were in the program. I worked to understand how to build a best-in-class program, which equated to the conversion of students to full-time employees and hiring a diverse group of students to support the innovation capability of the organization for the future. I reveled in the responsibility of helping college students start their careers. These possibilities in this role felt purposeful and meaningful as an homage to my unsettled feelings around not finding my dream role.

Unfortunately, the work of improving the program was only half the battle. I suffered for years under poor direction and management. There wasn't a term for 'gaslighting' at that time, but that was often my experience. I would call out a clear misstep and would be told that I was being 'too emotional' or not interpreting the situation correctly. I soldiered on, working harder, hoping that I would be deemed worthy in the eyes of my managers and co-workers. I internalized those moments of passive and direct aggression as indictments on my capability and worth. I suffered, often in silence, as I frequently experienced numerous 'isms' along the way: ageism in a department where I was one of the younger employees, sexism, as I was one of the few women in a male-dominated engineering environment, and racism. I wasn't prepared for this part of adulthood in corporate America. However, without being told, I knew or felt that there wasn't much I could do about my experiences without compromising my employment. I learned a lot the hard way, and my trust level in others' ability to support me or protect me from the worst behaviors by co-workers and leaders was nonexistent. My depressive funk continued, now with new confirmation that I wasn't good enough for respect or consideration in the workplace.

After a couple of years of feeling stranded in the middle of the ocean of adulthood, things started to perk up. I met my mentor, who became my best friend, while attending a networking function for business professionals. She was on a panel to share her experience about surviving in corporate America. Her honest and matter-of-fact nature seemed genuine, and I was moved to raise my hand to ask for help. This wasn't something I was doing very often. Up to that point, asking for help seemed to either elevate someone else or hurt me. Therefore, I did my best to stay hidden, even if it was to my detriment. This new relationship was a change to that trend almost immediately.

The best part about my new mentor was that she worked at the same company I did. Meeting her was transformative in many ways. To start with, she was the first person who validated my experiences and feelings and showed care and understanding of what I was going through. She affirmed that I wasn't crazy or to blame as she could relate to my experiences. Secondly, she didn't judge me and for once, I felt seen and valued. Third, she leveraged her role as a manager and helped me behind the scenes as I navigated my career for the remaining time I was there. Our friendship provided a reprieve to commiserate with safety and validation. As our friendship grew I was introduced to others like her and those friendships blossomed as well. These friendships provided a tribe of professional women where I could see that my experiences, as terrible as they were, were part of the journey in corporate America.

These friendships fortified me. I started borrowing on their belief in me to start believing in myself. I said "Yes" to trying new things like tennis, golf, and piano lessons. I started teaching high school students at a non-profit leadership program. I even moonlighted as a writer for a local entertainment paper, writing reviews of restaurants and personal essays. At work, opportunities would also pop up that I felt brave enough to say "Yes" to. I was a founding member of a young professionals employee resource group that ultimately won an award. I deepened my relationships with other non-profits, bringing their mission to my workplace. My friendships were the backbone of my growing confidence. These women frequently reminded me that I was smart and capable; I trusted them, and I started to trust myself.

Ultimately, I left this company after seven years and said "Yes" to a new opportunity as a management consultant. This transition presented a steeper learning curve than anticipated. I experienced many of the toxic behaviors that were present at the previous company: bullying, racism, sexism, and harassment. However, the stakes seemed higher as I navigated unique landmines of client politics, team dynamics, and project expectations. It was during this part of my career that some aspects started to crystallize. My desire for the grandiose titles, large amounts of responsibilities, and power was diminishing. I repeatedly saw that 'leader' didn't necessarily equate to a good and reputable person. Many of the leaders I encountered behaved badly; the way they treated others was repugnant and their professional values were not in alignment with mine. I understood the boundaries of my integrity and I knew that titles and organizational positioning were less important to me than I initially thought it would be. I started to reconsider how I would grow my career. Ultimately, I left this company after two and a half years for warmer weather and, more importantly, for love.

This transition proved to be a great opportunity for a shift in my career. At the time of the move, I was ten years into my career, in my early thirties, and feeling more sure of myself. I arrived in Houston, Texas, nervous and excited to create a reality for myself that felt more aligned to who I was becoming. I stayed in consulting and focused on mastering the skills for this career. I developed a strong understanding, aptitude, and ability to understand my clients' problems and provide options and approaches to solving those problems. I became a trusted advisor on projects and honed my ability to create and deliver high-quality client products. I harnessed my breadth of experiences and successfully applied the lessons and best practices to solving their problems.

This new decade of my career proved to be developing quite well. I was now serving in the role of mentor for younger employees. I stopped falling for the bait of doubt and uncertainty in my abilities and stayed laser-focused on what I did well and delivered accordingly. I accepted and promoted my superpower, my ability to execute well. It felt like the pieces were falling into place. I also got married during this time, and that action further focused me on what's really important. I had a family to think about, and the senseless behaviors of others affected me less. I felt braver than ever and decided to venture into the world of entrepreneurship. I started my first company, Plan Your Second Act, a consulting business for smaller businesses to coach their owners and streamline their operations. I did this while still working full-time.

My career was finally starting to make sense. What felt like a failure in the beginning was an ideal start for my ultimate life path. This is how I ended up at the front of Purdue University's Women's

Conference sharing a message of "The Power of Saying Yes." In the beginning, my first "Yes" was a disgruntled one. I felt shame and embarrassment starting my career in an industry I knew nothing about and a role that wasn't core to my abilities. I didn't celebrate this start as the accomplishment it was, and I didn't know that this start was part of being a lifelong learner. I gingerly stepped into the power of "Yes" with the friendships I made, the opportunities I accepted, and the activities I tried. They all served to cover the seeds of doubt, disappointment and shame I initially felt. The residue of *those* "Yeses" grew into opportunities I couldn't have imagined. International travel, decades-long friendships, and a breadth of experiences that I can confidently lean on to solve problems with familiarity and expertise.

It's interesting how the vision we have of ourselves is only half of what it takes to live the life of our dreams. Feeling like I mattered, having close ties and relationships, and resiliency, was the other half of living out the vision I had for my life. This vision didn't include the bumps and hard knocks that were a necessary part of my journey. It also didn't include the joy that I experienced along the way. What I didn't know at twenty-two was that life would make room for joy and pain; laughter and tears; and success and failure. It all serves the purpose of building up a strong and resilient person ready to take on new challenges with more confidence each and every day. Along the way I started to realize how "Yes" opened unexpected doors for me. While I didn't walk through all the open doors along the way, I discovered that saying "Yes" was my rainbow after a storm.

Today, I find myself looking for the next challenge. Most days, that challenge is being the best mother to my dynamic duo - a son and daughter and a loving wife to my wonderful husband. My friendships continue to anchor and support me as I take on new challenges in my lifelong journey of learning and curiosity. I'm stepping slowly back into the role of entrepreneur as I look to define how I want my future to look. I know for sure that my path of success is up to me to define, and my next opportunity is only one "Yes" away.

ABOUT THE AUTHOR

Tiffany M. Harris has twenty-plus years of expertise in leading Fortune 500 organizations through transformational changes. Her superpower is mastering the complexities of execution as businesses navigate through uncertainty and organizational change ,providing expertise in change management, learning, and project management.

Beyond her professional accomplishments, Tiffany cherishes most her family – husband, her dynamic twin duo. Her friendships continue to anchor and support her as she takes on new challenges in her lifelong journey of learning and curiosity. She's a storyteller, wanderlust, foodie, and wine enthusiast who calls Houston home. She's happiest exploring new places, writing for blogs and other outlets, podcasting, and preparing for her next travel adventure.

Her journey reflects both professional excellence, personal adventure and unyielding curiosity about what's next—allowing her to embrace the joy of discovery in her life.

@mrsbrowngirl10

LinkedIn: Tiffany M Harris

Chapter 14
Investing in Art
An Impactful Way to Grow Your Money
—Ann McCreath

The train was late arriving in Carlisle in the north of England. The ticket collector said they would hold the next train to Scotland at the station, but on arrival, it was nowhere to be seen. Instead, the Avanti staff asked us all to wait in a seating area and said they would be hiring taxis for us. I thought this would just be a regular taxi ride; little did I know I would gain a new perspective on my life and my unconventional investments.

So far, my trip had been flowing seamlessly. I was feeling in my "zen" mode after a few days in Bristol with my cousin. The day before, we had climbed St. Michael's Tor in Glastonbury, and then this morning I had met two dear friends in London for the Kerry James Marshall exhibition. He is an amazing African American artist who I had only recently discovered. His mammoth works were as much a skill in social commentary as they were in technique. The whole experience had left me super excited. As I walked around the Royal Academy, I wondered when some of the artists I knew in Kenya would make it this big. Wangeci Mutu, Michael Armitage and Kaloki Nyamai were already celebrated on the global stage. Many others had the talent, they just had to keep going, keep creating, so that they too would be "discovered."

We climbed in the cab, a young couple and I, and headed out on the motorway. It was a wild, rainy night with low visibility. I was used to male drivers in Nairobi; this time, it was a young Irish woman. After some general chat, she started to tell us her story. Her father and uncle had been top musicians in New York, and she had inherited their talent. She became an orphan when young and was separated from her siblings, but they had reunited as adults. She wanted to make a difference for other orphans, something that resonated with me. Where I lived, there were always people who needed a bit of help, and that assistance often blossomed into something extraordinary. Businesswomen like me seemed to naturally work social impact into their business models.

When I started my fashion brand, KikoRomeo, after many years of experience in Milan and Barcelona, I did so to create cash jobs for women and to give customers a ready-made garment they could take pride in. Something that told a story from fibre to finished product and could open conversations when worn on the global stage. I realized my expertise was quite unique in Kenya and knew that the handcrafted quality could fetch higher prices if the design and finishing were good. I had trained in couture in Rome, even working as a tailor, and so I could sit at a machine and teach specific garment-making techniques, as well as organize a fashion show or a photoshoot. I had worked across all aspects of the fashion industry, so it was easy for me to see what could be improved and how. I could advise clients on what to wear for which occasion and, in so doing, help them navigate the echelons of power designed to keep some people out of the top layer of decision-making.

Our conversation was fascinating. She worked remotely in tech, highly qualified in a specialized field. She and her partner were planning to go to Georgia, apparently a fast-growing tech hub, where you could earn big money. I asked her why she was doing Uber in addition to a remote job. She was raising money for her own business – she wanted to employ other young people like herself. She told us she had invested in gold, silver, and crypto. I had never met someone like this – I wondered out loud where she stored her gold. *"It's just at home in the safe"*, she said. She and her partner had keys. I hoped her partner was genuine and kind; my experience in trusting men had not always been successful. I pondered what her gold looked like – I had just visited the Museo del Oro in Bogotá, Colombia, which was filled with the most beautiful golden treasures – jewelry, decorations, and artefacts. I didn't think I had seen a gold nugget before, sure and safe in its rectangular solidity, quite different from these delicate, intricate pieces, but shiny and the same magnificent colour. We discussed her investments for a while. The other two in the back joined the conversation, and then one of them turned to me and asked, *"What have you invested in?"*

I thought for a moment, I started saying *"I haven't really..."* and then checked myself. I had been doing a lot of self-awareness work and many courses on my relationship with money, and how to talk about it. I knew I wasn't supposed to say anything negative about me and it. We were to flow in harmony. My mind wandered off into my journey with pranic healing, becoming a healer and then getting healing myself as I considered how to respond to my fellow passengers. Money. In venturing deeper and deeper into pranic healing, I had helped many women who had been abused, sexually abused. At some point, I realized this had happened to me. In this process of self-discovery, I started to read more about the effects of such early trauma. It was all there as if my life had been scripted. Abuse leading to a lack of self-worth, low self-esteem, and the ego helping you to keep going, even though underneath was extremely fragile. And therefore money. Not saving it – over the years, I had been very successful, made a lot, and spent it quickly. Spending it on everyone else first, myself last, just as I had always done in my business. I was always the last to get paid, and yet I was the person driving the ideas, the fabulous creations and bringing in the business. How would I ever have invested anything? And then I remembered where I was and blurted out, *"Actually, I have invested! Not in an orthodox way that accountants would advise you to do, but in my way, in a way that brought me joy."* I realised that over the years I had invested bit by bit in works of art that meant something to me. Pieces that were often created by another soul, whose story resonated with me as well as their creativity.

They were intrigued. I told them about my art collection. I had always loved art. I studied History of Art at the University of Edinburgh and travelled all over Europe, looking at cathedrals and museums when I was younger. My cousin Michael Johnson, now a famous painter, stayed with me for a while in Barcelona and gave me one of his pieces. It had disappeared from my house when I travelled, alongside my fashion portfolio, an annoying confirmation that art has a tangible value. Then, when I lived in Angola in 1990 and afterwards in Kenya, I used any disposable money from my NGO jobs to buy art. Having connected to the art world, I realised that making a living from fashion would be much more fun so I set up my own fashion brand in 1996.

On the production side, I quickly found being an entrepreneur far more satisfying personally than working in relief aid. I could see the craftswomen were so excited to have a market for the beautiful things they made by hand. They could also make them easily at home while doing household chores and caring for their children. To ensure garment consistency, I set up a workshop and handled the pattern cutting, but the handwork on leather or cloth was done through women's groups. I would go to their rural locations, so we could figure out together how to create my designs. Such handicrafts are also art, and they too carry the love of the person crafting. I loved including them in our pieces.

I started thinking about how we could integrate more art into fashion. I organized our first real show at the French Cultural Centre in 1998. I didn't want to copy the European runway style, but I did want to have excellent quality production. So I commissioned artist Mazola wa Mwashighadi to do the stage décor and Hot Rod Band to play live music. This started a trend of exciting events, which are ingrained in the memories of Nairobians. Our first proper shop was designed by already renowned sculptor Kioko Mwitiki together with architect and artist Kahare Miano and Ali Mwangola. It was funky, it was different. Huge metal guitar sculptures towered above the cash desk with music blaring out of one of them. They became the talk of the town, with people coming just to experience the space. I started collaborating with visual artist Eltayeb Dawelbait, a newcomer to town from Sudan, to develop unique textiles in a partnership that has lasted more than two decades. I also collaborated with photographers such as Robert Maletta and Emmanuel Jambo, writers including the late Binyavanga Wainaina, and musicians such as Suzanna Owiyo, Eric Wainaina, Nameless, and Blinky Bill. Art in the widest sense has always been at the forefront of the KikoRomeo brand.

Every time there was an opportunity to acquire art, I bought or bartered for it. I can't live without art; it brings me immense joy. It's more than just a decoration on a wall; it's a living energy, a higher vibration, which permeates the space. It's as if all the love that the artist poured into the work is held within that canvas, in the colours and the stroke of the brush. During an earlier period of political turmoil in Kenya, I realized that, aside from my family, friends, and pets, all I really cared about was art. I had thought through what I would flee with, how I would carefully remove it from the wooden frame, fold it and pack it. Mine was a different reality from the three who were gripped by my story. I had lived near war zones and worked with refugees, and so such unimaginable scenarios took on very realistic dimensions for me. My thoughts returned to the present; art was my gold. I had an amazing collection; if I ever sold it all, I could buy an apartment.

They were impressed. They had never thought about art as an investment. We started talking about how museums and galleries are often the first things to be pillaged in times of war, with works resurfacing decades later. Hiding art from the Nazis in Italy and the film about it.The recent pillaging of the Museum in Khartoum and its invaluable ancient artefacts. I had done a photoshoot there before the war of the designs of my Sudanese fashion designer mentees. Such photos could never be replicated. We had filmed them just before everything collapsed. I thought of Syria and the destruction of so many ancient sites, Iraq, and now Iran and Palestine. The list went on and on. You see, art is valuable beyond money. It is the root of our culture, the essence of our being, the force to fight back. Without it, we become lost, disoriented and lacking in confidence. Just as a child with low self-esteem becomes disoriented, a population without its culture becomes disoriented. It is what connects us to our heritage, and to our Soul and so it is the first thing destroyed when an invading power wants to control the population.

They asked me how I knew what to buy. I thought about my actual collection pieces and what had drawn me to them. Generally, I like abstract art, often figurative. I have never gone for realism, because I find the story scripted; it leaves less room for my imagination. Instead, I have been driven to buy colours, textures and concepts. Paintings that move me emotionally, harmonious compositions, boldness. Thick to thin paint, washed out areas, voids where imagination takes over and fills in the dots. Paintings, which allow me to always see something different, layers of meaning. Some tell political stories of their time, always with a spiritual angle. Contrasting colours which inadvertently inform fabric choices for our KikoRomeo collections, as they are lodged in the back of my being, just by sharing the same space.

Reflecting on my collection from an investment perspective, the artists I bought from were already exhibiting in art galleries of one kind or another. Eltayeb was well known in Sudan and later moved to Kenya. Mazola had moved to the capital, Nairobi, from the Coast, to be closer to his customers. My recent acquisitions included some from Galal, who was at the forefront of the people's revolution in Khartoum, Sudan. Kenyan luminary Onyis Martin and his painting featuring the Kenyan Nobel Peace Prize winner Wangari Maathai, my dear friend Kiboko and the largest part of his *"Kata-Kata"* canvas, which he cut up at my *#Annskitchen* dinner nearly a decade before. All the artists I had chosen were artists on the move, philosophers with a lot to say, people determined to make the world a better place. They had a beautiful vision and were activists through their art. They had ambition, often hidden from the regular stock-exchange buyer by dreadlocks, and wanted to make a mark on the world. They rarely had much money, but they knew one day they would. They were all in it for the passion, just like me.

Over the years, I introduced artists I liked to other buyers. I took my friends to exhibitions, and they bought too. Connecting people around my dinner table was always such fun and an accidental way to help these artists become better known, as interesting conversations often led to art sales. Reflecting back on this, I realise that the more an artist becomes known, the more their prices go up, and so it's in every art buyer's interest to promote those you buy from. On the business side, KikoRomeo dressed artists for their opening shows, which was great for our brand. Our outfits were also guaranteed to build confidence at such an important moment, when the artist had to introduce their work and wait for the critics to have their say.

In a country like Kenya, where there is little-to-no official safety net for anyone unemployed or sick, families step in. Primary education is heavily subsidised, and then from high school onwards, you have to pay. Most employees have a side business to earn a bit more cash to supplement their salaries. Everyone is supporting a network of less fortunate friends or relatives. Artists are no exception; they, too, have many people who depend on them beyond the nuclear family. Those who make it big often start projects to help others, such as NCAI (Nairobi Contemporary Art Institute) and the Kamene Centre. There are even NGOs that specialise in giving youth a space to paint and connecting them to art markets. Buying art literally supports communities.

When I realised the monetary value of my collection, I started to buy paintings for my family as presents. While in Ethiopia, I bought a small one by Dawit Abebe; it was worth much more just 5 years later, when he started holding solo exhibitions globally. For my daughter's birthday, I commissioned a portrait by a young Kenyan artist, Rasto Ciprian, who, less than 2 years later, had his first solo at a top gallery in Nairobi. Now she, too, has a growing art collection and many artist friends with whom she can barter or buy from. Unlike generations of parents before me, I think being an artist is a very valid career choice.

Thinking back on the money I invested and what it is worth now, it has been an amazing investment. Most of the pieces have appreciated 10-15 times the initial purchase price over 10-20 years, and they give me so much joy to look at every day. The method of acquiring the pieces has always included interesting conversations and little pressure. The result of my acquisition has always contributed to dinner-party discussions about the work and its creator, often with him or her present. And while I might not want to sell my pieces right now, there are many commercial gallerists, collectors, and the Nairobi Art Auction, all of which offer opportunities to sell. Even the artists of the pieces themselves, who have made it with solo shows, sometimes buy back their own art to show it in retrospective exhibitions and sell it for profit. In such an environment, art is a low-risk investment with pieces which can be gifted or sold at any time. It's never too late to start.

As I parted ways with my fellow travellers, I took great pleasure in realising that my gut feeling about buying art was actually a clever way to make a lasting investment.

ABOUT THE AUTHOR

Ann McCreath lives in Nairobi, Kenya and is the founder of fashion heritage brand KikoRomeo. Born in Scotland, she set up her fashion brand in Kenya in 1996 to generate income for women and celebrate handcrafted techniques in clothing. She is a pioneer in sustainable fashion. She has an MA from the University of Edinburgh, a first-class Diploma in Fashion from KOEFIA in Rome and over three decades of experience in the fashion industry.

Since 2018, McCreath has been a lead consultant on international fashion development programs. She has written fashion curricula for designers and tailors across Africa, training over 500 to date. She continues to mentor these designers and foster peer-learning through WhatsApp groups, which also promote intra-African business connections. She has also developed short fashion courses for refugees and, in the process, discovered the wealth of crafts and cultures in the bustling Kakuma refugee camp. In 2020, she developed courses for 130 tailors in the disadvantaged neighbourhoods of Kampala and Nairobi. Covering fashion branding and mask-making for UN Women and the IOM, the Nairobi project generated 57,000 pieces in Nairobi alone.

She serves on the advisory board of Building African Fashion and is currently establishing a Fashion Innovation Lab for designers in Nairobi.

Instagram: @annmccreath @kikoromeo

Chapter 15
Beyond Transactions
The Art of Giving in Business
—Alexandra Yung

In a world defined by fierce competition, particularly for small businesses, the path to success often seems riddled with cut-throat tactics. As entrepreneurs, we must navigate a landscape where customers are inundated with choices, all vying for attention through claims of quality, craftsmanship, and value. Yet, through my own experiences, I've discovered a timeless truth that serves as my guiding light: it's not about selling; but about giving.

Throughout my journey, I have been blessed with gifts that come in innumerable forms, gifts that extend far beyond financial wealth. The invaluable treasures of time, wisdom, insights, kindness, and love have all played a crucial role in shaping my identity and in creating the foundation of my work. These offerings have woven the fabric of my soul, propelling me forward as a female entrepreneur navigating the complexities of business and life.

Even in moments of struggle, perceived setbacks often morphed into profound lessons. Each challenge I faced has become a stepping stone to growth, shedding light on the beauty of resilience and the transformative power of a giving spirit.

True giving is rooted in selflessness and free of any agendas and expectations. I vividly recall an early job experience where I took a bold leap of faith: I worked without pay for an entire month to showcase my value to a company as I really wanted to work for this organization. I didn't have the right experience and qualifications they were looking for, but I knew that if I can show them what I can do, I can show my value. My gamble paid off; before the month ended, I secured a full-time position and also re-confirmed my desire to join the company. This experience taught me that when you offer your talents freely, new opportunities can emerge. If working for an entire month isn't feasible, even a week or two can allow you to demonstrate your abilities and assess whether the position aligns with your expectations.

As an artist, I've always derived immense joy from using my creative talents as gifts. I remember creating paintings and artworks but never sold them and ended up giving them away to friends and family. Each piece is not just an expression of my artistic vision, but also a reflection of my feelings, carrying my vibrations and energy. Gifting these creations was far more gratifying than selling them for monetary gain; it strengthened my bond with others and allowed me to share a part of myself through my art. Hand-made gifts carry a special significance, as they represent something from the heart that money can't buy. In fact it was only in recent years that I began to sell my own art for money.

My journey as a master energy healer further highlights the transformative power of giving. Although trained as a Sekhem energy master, I had never taught or used my healing professionally. I used the training as a way to develop my own personal growth and strengthen my spiritual connection. However, I was on a trip in Italy years ago when a woman twisted her ankle badly; upon seeing her hobbling around in pain, I felt compelled to help. Using my healing energy on her ankle, I seemed to have expedited her recovery, and by that night, she was dancing with joy. In that moment, there was no monetary transaction; however, I experienced an overwhelming sense of fulfillment and pride that I was able to help someone in need. Contributing to her well-being proved to be more valuable than any form of compensation, reinforcing my belief that genuine giving often results in a tenfold return, not in currency, but in gratitude, joy, and connection.

Being creative is my lifelong passion. Besides painting and ceramics, it extends into photography and video production. Creating videos for events, small businesses, or communities has become another canvas for my creativity. When I offer these services pro bono, I experience a profound sense of achievement. My work captures fleeting moments and timeless memories that might otherwise be forgotten, sharing them with the world.

Engaging in acts of service is among the most fulfilling ways to give, as it is something no amount of money can buy. I find that whether I'm lending a hand at an event, volunteering at a local charity, or supporting a friend in need, the deep joy of serving is incomparable. Volunteering at seminars and workshops and witnessing transformations in attendees has proven to be profoundly rewarding, again reinforcing my belief that giving gets rewarded ten-fold.

As I embark on my latest business venture, a private lifestyle hub specializing in bio-hacking technologies and culinary arts for well-being. This journey feels like my ultimate legacy, my passion project. I believe health is the cornerstone of life. Without health, enjoying life to the fullest becomes impossible. Even with all the money in the world, we cannot savor joy. My idea was sparked by the impact of COVID and the undeniable fact that many friends face health issues like high blood pressure, high cholesterol, diabetes, and more. As I age, I, too, face health challenges, notably my gluten intolerance, which necessitates a strict diet. At the same time, I refuse to forgo the pleasures of good food. Thus, I envisioned a venue that offers exceptional, delicious dishes fit for connoisseurs, all while embodying healthy preparation methods. People can truly relish a full life without sacrificing their joys or their favorite foods. We even ensure that the alcohol offered is organic and biodynamic, containing fewer chemicals and sulfites, to enhance enjoyment without compromising health.

My vision is to create a space in Hong Kong, and potentially the world, where individuals can fully

embrace life while prioritizing their health. We provide unique and delicious cuisines, crafted from the finest ingredients and adhering to rigorous health standards—free from refined sugars, wheat, and preservatives; low in carbs, fat, and salt; utilizing heart-healthy oils from micro-algae. Every dish is meticulously designed to blend originality with ingredients from my global travels. To me, food transcends mere taste; it's an experience that engages all senses. Each plate serves as my canvas, where the visual presentation tantalizes before the first bite. Evoking all the senses of sight, smell, taste and feel accompanied by music makes the experience a total immersive one, making it a memorable event.

Venturing into a unique business model comes with inherent risks. While consumers may gravitate toward established establishments with predictable offerings, it's essential to build trust for differentiation. People engage with businesses because of the relationships they foster, not merely the brand itself.

In the lifestyle hub, we offer tastings at little to no cost and invite clients to experience the magic of our offerings firsthand. This goes beyond mere sampling; it's about crafting experiences that create lasting positive emotions. Guests leave enchanted, becoming brand ambassadors, referral partners, and lifelong loyalists, returning not out of obligation but out of choice. This strategy echoes my early gamble of working for free: give a taste, prove your worth, and watch reciprocity unfold.

Even if you're not in a position to give away products or services, effective marketing, branding, and sales are investments every business must make. Tasting products, much like tasting wine or sampling food at fairs, leads to personal connections that drive purchases. Just as movie trailers offer a glimpse of the movie as an enticement to pay for the whole movie, businesses often benefit from trials that enhance conversion rates.

One of my favorite quotes encapsulates the essence of opportunity: "If you give someone a fish, you feed them for a day. If you teach them how to fish, you feed them for a lifetime." The most valuable gift lies not just in the fish or the lesson, but in the opportunity to discover one's own capabilities.

Opportunities shape self-perception. Providing someone with money might offer a temporary fix, but handing over an opportunity communicates something far more powerful: belief. You're acknowledging, "I see potential in you. I trust you with this responsibility. I believe you can rise to the occasion." This belief can be life-altering, planting a seed that blossoms into confidence, ownership, and self-respect.

Through my experiences, I've found that when given genuine chances, most people can exceed expectations, especially when they feel supported rather than rescued. Growth flourishes when individuals are invited to take on responsibility. This is why I prefer creating energy exchanges rather than handouts. An exchange, whether of work, effort, or expertise fosters equality and keeps the energy flowing. It creates an environment where both parties show up with dignity and commitment, making growth a mutual endeavor.

When individuals earn their progress, something remarkable happens: they take ownership. They protect what they've cultivated and push themselves further because their success is not simply granted, borrowed, or dependent on anyone else. The opportunity becomes a mirror reflecting their untapped potential.

Having run several businesses, I've observed this transformation repeatedly. When someone is entrusted with responsibility, they often rise up to the occasion. When taught rather than rescued, they become resourceful. When offered ownership instead of mere instructions, they evolve into leaders. Opportunity unveils potential that even individuals may be unaware exists. Of course there is always someone who is the exception to this rule and attitude is also a huge factor in their success.

In my current venture, I collaborated with a few friends who contributed complementary strengths. Some of my team members may not have the financial means to invest, yet this opportunity enables them to grow alongside the business. They contribute their time and expertise while experiencing ownership in our cause. Even staff members who receive a salary feel like an integral part of the team, as they get to sample our latest innovative dishes or try our latest therapies. They aren't merely working for money; they are part of something greater, experiencing the holistic vision and impact that I am creating. At the same time, it is also an opportunity for them to be healthier.

Creating opportunities isn't always straightforward. It requires patience, mentorship, and the courage to allow others to stumble and learn from their mistakes. The long-term effects are immeasurable; you are not just helping someone overcome a hurdle today; you are equipping them to construct a sustainable future. It also makes me more tolerant as I bite my lips to deal with frustrations and disappointments when deadlines are missed and things go wrong.

This is the giving that multiplies. One opportunity can shift a mindset, and a changed mindset can transform a life. A transformed life often goes on to create opportunities for others and impact expands beyond finances and into the realm of empowerment.

For me, true giving means not saving people but strengthening them. It encompasses not providing answers but facilitating discovery. The greatest gift is the chance for someone to achieve greatness and to know deeply and unapologetically that they accomplished it.

Reflecting on my journey, I can truly say that each act of giving, every moment I chose to assist, share expertise, or lend my strength has yielded returns tenfold or greater. These rewards take countless forms: friendships forged, new opportunities discovered, and the joy of witnessing others succeed.

As I continue down this path, I remain steadfast in my commitment to the philosophy of giving. Each lesson learned and every story shared enriches my life and those I touch. In both business and life, giving isn't just as important as receiving, it's the ultimate multiplier. By focusing on uplifting others, we inevitably uplift ourselves in the process.

True transformation arises from the magic of giving, cultivating an interconnected community that uplifts each member. This cycle strengthens our understanding that giving leads to receiving in ways that surpass our expectations, resulting in richer, more fulfilling experiences for everyone involved.

As a business owner, I've often confronted the vulnerability of letting go, allowing team members to rise, even when my instincts urge caution. This has been a difficult lesson for me. Understanding that empowering others may require stepping back and observing them, sometimes allowing them to make mistakes to learn the hard way. There were moments of doubt, worrying that their choices could lead to missteps. Yet, I realized that enabling them to face these challenges is essential for their growth.

The choice of whom to work with is one of the most empowering decisions any business owner can make. Surrounding yourself with givers, those who share talents, uplift others, and foster collective growth creates powerful synergy. These are the individuals who understand the significance of collaboration, igniting creativity and innovation.

Conversely, it's vital to distance yourself from takers, those who may drain energy and resources without reciprocating. Building a team of givers not only strengthens your organization but fosters a thriving environment for all.

Seeking feedback and being open to customer suggestions are critical for business success. Delivering what people truly want not only fosters loyalty but establishes genuine connections. Embracing a philosophy of giving revolutionizes customer relations, elevating interactions from transactional to deeply relational.

In summary, my entrepreneurial philosophy advocates for the delicate balance of asserting authority and allowing others to take charge. This balance demands confidence in my vision, alongside acute sensitivity to team dynamics.

Sometimes, significant progress arises from embracing risky suggestions especially when my instincts lean toward caution. Building a business alongside a team of friends invites unique challenges yet can culminate in extraordinary collaborations built on mutual respect.

By nurturing an environment where every team member feels valued and empowered, we enhance collaboration, igniting growth and innovation. Our shared experiences both frustrations and triumphs, transform into a powerful narrative of success. This intricate dance of leadership, knowing when to guide and when to step back, defines a thriving business culture and leaves a lasting legacy.

In building a more compassionate world, my wish is for everyone to embrace the transformative power of giving. In this act, we cultivate mutually beneficial relationships, propelling both our personal and professional lives toward a more connected and sustainable future.

ABOUT THE AUTHOR

Alexandra Yung is a multifaceted creative professional who began her career in the US before pioneering the Internet industry in Hong Kong, where she led a creative team to secure a landmark US$50 million investment through innovative branding.

In 2002, she founded Creasians, introducing her unique approach, Brandology, which blends branding with emotional engagement. Her work has successfully branded individuals, products, and even a city in China. As Managing Director of a boutique auction house and art gallery, she organized significant events and ventured into the crypto space, facilitating early NFT transactions.

A passionate artist and master energy healer, Alexandra developed the E-motion series—mixed media artworks on canvas that incorporate oil paints and essential oils infused with healing energy. Additionally, she creates intricate hand-drawn mandalas utilizing sacred geometry, promoting mindfulness and spiritual growth.

In addition to her artistic pursuits, Alexandra has recently launched a Lifestyle Hub that combines her passions of wellness with bio-hacking sensory experiences and wellness-focused cuisine, dedicated to curating transformative experiences that positively impact lives.

www.creasians.com

www.cre8tif.art

IG: alexandra_yung

Thank You

Enjoyed *Femme Led*?

Your feedback means the world to us!

If the book resonated with you, inspired you, or offered some-thing meaningful, we'd truly appreciate it if you left a **review on Amazon** or **GoodReads**. Your feedback helps others discover the book—and it directly supports the author's work.

Acknowledgments

Every book is the result of many hands and hearts. An anthology, even more so. The book you hold is the result of the devotion, courage, and generosity of the authors, along with the mentors, editors, and supporters who helped bring these stories to life.

Carol Britton and **Dr. Katherine Humphreys** served not only as contributing authors but also as mentors to this group. Their thoughtful attention, guidance, and encouragement helped shape each chapter.

Editors are often the invisible contributors behind every great book. **Mimi Rich** and **Stacy Dyson** worked carefully to refine and polish these chapters, helping each author bring forward her strongest voice and clearest message.

The vision and steady leadership of **Sierra Melcher**, CEO of Red Thread Publishing, has been the backbone of this project, creating the collaborative process and supportive environment that allowed these authors to do this work together.

What we hope you remember is this: these pages carry the lived experience, uncomfortable truths, and wisdom of many remarkable people. None of us creates alone. But together, we create something far greater than any one voice.

ABOUT THE PUBLISHER

Red Thread Publishing is an award-winning indie press dedicated to amplifying powerful, authentic nonfiction voices. In our first five years, we've published more than 75 books, supported over 400 authors from 31 countries, and celebrated 52 book awards, proof of the impact and quality behind every title we produce.

Our passionate team is committed to guiding authors through every step of the writing and publishing journey so their stories not only get published but make a lasting impact.

If you want to **write & publish with us** please reach out.
Visit **www.redthreadbooks.com**
Email us **info@redthreadbooks.com**

instagram.com/redthreadbooks
facebook.com/redthreadpublishing
linkedin.com/company/red-thread-publishing

Other Books
Find Your Next Favorite Read

RED THREAD ANTHOLOGIES

~

The Split

This anthology dismantles generations of stigma around divorce and womanhood, replacing it with a message of renewal, courage, and collective healing. These are not broken women. They are bold, audacious, and resilient—choosing themselves, their peace, and a new path forward. *Splitting isn't the end; it's a rebirth*

Winner of the American Writing Awards 2025

~

Taboo: Stories That Can't Be Told

Unflinching yet intimate, *Taboo: Stories That Can't Be Told* gathers voices that give language to pain, prejudice, and resilience—inviting us to dismantle the walls of silence we build around the unspeakable.

Winner of the American Legacy Book Awards, Firebird Awards and Literary Titan Book Awards 2025

Planting the Seed: Lessons to Cultivate a Brighter Future

Planting the Seed weaves together intimate, courageous stories from women who have faced deep adversity—infidelity, illness, injustice, and more—and emerged resilient, wise, and ready to grow. Each narrative is a seed of hope, offering lessons in strength, transformation, and the promise of a brighter tomorrow.

Winner of the Nautilus Book Award: Silver Prize in Rising to the Moment 2024

Sactuary: Cultivating Safe Space in Sisterhood; Rediscovering the Power that Unites Us

Sanctuary presents vivid narratives of vulnerability and restoration, showing how sisterhood can become a sacred space where women reclaim voice, belonging, and collective strength.

Winner of Finalist in the American Writing Awards 2024

SPARK: Women in the Business of Changing the World

is a powerful collection of voices from women across the globe, sharing how they're leading with purpose, ambition, and heart.

Winner of the Bronze Global Book Awards, Women in Business 2025

Notes From Motherland: The Wild Adventure of Raising Humans

In *Notes From Motherland*, each story serves as a window into the unpredictable journey of raising children—navigating hope, heartbreak, growth, and resilience in the day-to-day.

Winner of the Literary Titan Book Awards 2024

FEISTY: Dangerously Amazing Women Using Their Voices & Making An Impact

Bold, raw, and unapologetic, *FEISTY* invites readers into the fire of female power, spotlighting voices that demand to be heard—and showing how courage becomes impact.

Winner of the Literary Titan Book Awards 2025

MENtal Health: Take it "Like a Man"

In *MENtal Health: Take It "Like a Man"*, each narrative becomes a courageous testimony, unfiltered and raw, challenging traditional ideas of masculinity by showing how vulnerability and recovery are essential steps toward wholeness.

Winner of the Literary Titan Book Awards 2025

The Anatomy of a Book

A definitive guide for aspiring authors, featuring insights from 20 industry veterans on writing, publishing, and book marketing. Whether you're new to writing or aiming to elevate your publishing efforts, this anthology offers practical, behind-the-scenes wisdom to help bring your book into the world.

Winner of International Impact Book Awards 2025

By the Light of the Moon

A luminous anthology of personal stories from women who lean into the power and mystery of the feminine.

Winner of the Firebird Awards 2024

Typo: The Art of Imperfect Creation

A compassionate guide for writers, giving you permission to embrace messiness as you begin your story. It offers exercises, insights, and encouragement to help you transform what feels broken or chaotic into something meaningful, daring, and uniquely your own.

Winner of the Nautilus Book Award: Gold Prize in Creativity and Innovation 2024